THE POWER OF PURPOSE

ISBN (paperback): 9781960111289

Library of Congress Number: 2025904222

THE POWER OF PURPOSE

A GUIDE TO HELP YOU DISCOVER YOURS

MITCH LARSON

For Tamela, who has filled my life with purpose.

CONTENTS

FOREWORD

LINDSAY BEDNAR

There are people you meet in life who come at just the right time, with the right energy, reminding you how alignment works. Had I met Mitch ten, or even five, years earlier, I wouldn't have been able to serve him through this book in the way I can now. I had more to learn and more lessons to absorb. I'm also not sure our connection would have been as strong or as essential to my evolution in how I see and operate in the world. The timing was divine. This project made me shout, "Absolutely yes!" and deepened my desire to be around Mitch and bring this book to life.

To me, there is no greater task in life than finding your purpose—it's the sole (or should I say soul) reason we're all here. I've experienced firsthand how magnificent life becomes once you discover and deepen your purpose, which you'll read more about later in this book. So, when Mitch approached me with his book idea and the intention behind it, I was intrigued. But as I learned more about who he is and how he leads his life, my answer became a resounding yes. Many can talk theoretically about the power of purpose, but not everyone lives it day by day. Knowing your purpose is vital; living it makes all the difference.

Creating this book with Mitch has been an incredibly fulfilling and rewarding experience. I am confident you'll appreciate the simplicity of the framework, the engaging journal prompts, and, above all, his unique ability to share life experiences in both touching and humorous ways. My sincere hope is that you find your unique purpose and ultimately lead a life of service and deep personal fulfillment.

INTRODUCTION

Welcome! Thank you for investing in yourself and your future! Over the past thirty years, I've focused on helping individuals enhance their most valuable asset: themselves.

As a lifelong learner, I'm an avid reader of personal and professional self-development books and regularly listen to audiobooks and podcasts on the same topic. I have authored several articles for a variety of publications and speak regularly in front of a wide variety of audiences. This is my first book and I am so glad you picked it up.

Like so many others, I have always desired to write a book but didn't know how to take it from an idea to a finished marketable product. Enter Rodney K Press and Lindsay Bednar. I met Lindsay through her husband Gary, an associate and friend. He and I were on the golf course a few years ago when, in passing, I mentioned my desire to write a book. He smiled and said that he might know someone who could help me with that. He was talking about Lindsay, whose company does just that. You will learn more about Rodney K Press publishing and Lindsay's purpose in a later chapter.

I wrote this book because I've observed a significant difference in the quality and content of life between those people who have identified and actively pursued a purpose for their lives and those who let life direct them without clear intention. Just the other day, I heard someone say, "Well, I just go where life takes me." No offense to that individual, but I am convinced that we are created and designed for more.

So many people share the common experience of achieving financial success or attaining a particular rank, title, or position within their chosen profession only to find they are still unfulfilled.

Helping people identify and develop their purpose is *my* purpose and why you are holding this book in your hands. Within it, I share my lifelong journey of discovering and developing my purpose, featuring stories and examples from childhood to the present, along with the tools that have helped me along the way. I'm confident that when you understand and apply what I've shared, you too will be able to identify and develop your true purpose.

I wouldn't be authentic if I didn't mention in this introduction that the confidence, belief, and content for this book is a direct result of my walk with my Lord and Savior, Jesus. He has directed and guided me in the form of my still small voice and has brought along the right people and resources at exactly the right time—truly the fingerprints of God.

I reside in Shakopee, Minnesota, with Tamela, my wonderful wife of more than forty years. When I'm not working, I'm an (average) avid golfer and snowmobiler. I love music, singing, and playing the guitar, and you'll find me pulling for my favorite teams: the Minnesota Twins, the Minnesota Wild, and the Green Bay Packers (sorry, I was born and raised in Wisconsin). Now, please don't hate me—at least acknowledge the courage it took for me to put this in my introduction, living in Minnesota. I also love traveling, exploring new places, and spending time with my ever-growing family.

May you enjoy reading and applying this book as much as I have enjoyed bringing it from idea and concept to reality!

"THE MEANING OF LIFE IS TO HELP OTHERS
FIND THE MEANING OF THEIRS."
— Victor Frankl (1905-1997), *Man's Search for Meaning*

WHAT IS PURPOSE?

There are two monumental days in everyone's life: the day they're born and the day they discover why. In this book, I will provide you with a guide that will help you uncover your true purpose in life, learn how to access that purpose, and provide you with the tools needed to pursue it.

I submit that many people never achieve their dreams and goals because they fail to clearly define their purpose in life. The two are perfectly and inexplicably intertwined—you can't have one without the other. This book will help you define, develop, and accomplish yours. My objective is to help you discover the well of energy and power that lies within and understand that you are fully able, regardless of your age or circumstances, to identify and fulfill your purpose in life.

Webster defines the noun *purpose* as "the reason for which something is done or created or for which something exists." Such is the power of purpose. Purpose provides clarity where there is confusion, motivation where there is a lack of motivation, direction if we are lost, and determination and persistence to stay the course.

THERE ARE DIFFERENT TYPES OF PURPOSE:

- **Immediate** - I need to get to the grocery store because we don't have enough food for everyone coming over today!
- **Short-term** - I need to lose thirty pounds on this sixty-day program. If I don't follow this program closely, it won't work.
- **Long-term** - Now that I've lost the weight, I need to modify my eating and exercise to avoid gaining it all back.
- **Lifelong or overarching** - There is something that I am set to accomplish in this life. It is up to me—if I don't do it, it won't get done. This is what this book will help you identify.

That's a key descriptor of your true purpose: What can only you, with your special set of talents, abilities, and gifts, do?

This book focuses on your lifelong, overarching purpose. It will provide clarity for your life and help you become all you are designed to be. I'm confident in the truth of this statement because I am living proof. The idea for this book germinated in my mind decades ago as I became more involved in adult education and training because of the various jobs I was doing. I began to see more and more people limiting their true and full potential because of the limits they were imposing on themselves. While this book is a guide to help you find your purpose, it is also equally as much a compilation of tools and techniques to help you unlock your full potential.

GOALS

VISION

PURPOSE

PURPOSE PYRAMID

"PURPOSE IS THE FOUNDATIONAL BEDROCK TO ALL
ACCOMPLISHMENTS IN LIFE. WITH IT, MOUNTAINS CAN
BE MOVED; WITHOUT IT, THE SMALLEST OF OBSTACLES
WILL STOP YOU."

Purpose answers the all-important question of "Why?"—the driving force behind every action, decision, and pursuit. Any good detective will tell you that once the 'why' becomes clear, the puzzle begins to solve itself. The "who," "what," "where," and "when" naturally align, revealing patterns and connections that seemed elusive before. Another way to explain "why" is "motive," the reasons behind our existence and the decisions we make. Why am I here? Why does this matter? Purpose gives these questions meaning, acting as a lens that brings our life into sharper focus. With purpose, we not only see the road ahead but also value in the journey itself, guiding us to act with intention and clarity.

Mission and vision statements—for individuals and organizations alike—are rooted in purpose. A mission statement is a simple, effective statement of your purpose, without which you would have no mission. For example, my church's mission statement is this: "To know Christ and make Him known." I love this mission statement because it is simple, clear, and completely on purpose. When you read it, you know what the church is about.

Goals and objectives are also anchored in purpose. Once you know what you want to do, goal-setting is the tool that breaks purpose into manageable, attainable chunks. Goals help you stay on task, generate momentum, and keep you moving forward. It's like the old adage: How do you eat an elephant? One bite at a time.

Let's use this book as an example. While the process of writing and publishing a book can easily take years, I wrote and published this book in nine months. How did that happen? First, God showed me the purpose of this book: to help others find their purpose and make a difference in His Kingdom. As this vision began to take shape in my mind, I could see the title and outline of the book. My mission was clear: to complete the book and launch a speaking business. From there, as mentioned in the introduction, God led me to Rodney K Press and Lindsay, who has extensive publishing experience.

While creating the book, I am simultaneously identifying and connecting with key individuals, industries, and audiences who can benefit from my message and mentoring. This effort not only allows me to add value to their lives but also helps establish myself as a speaker and mentor during the process.

While living a life on purpose is the focus of this book, I'd be remiss if I didn't examine the opposite side of the equation and discuss my observations on lives lived without purpose. It has become clear to me that if you don't intentionally give your mind a purpose, it will find one on its own—and that purpose is often unhealthy. I believe this observation is vital and needs to be discussed.

You don't have to look very far to find the people in your life who lack purpose. Whether it's a family member, friend, or someone you work with, you can easily identify them because they often share a number of the same recognizable traits. First, let's look at the image below. The arrows represent a person's focus. Their arrows are pointed inward, focusing only on themselves. This can lead to an increase in anxiety and stress, stagnation, and missed opportunities.

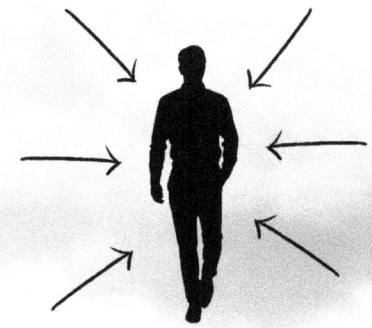

SELF-FOCUSED

Individuals living without purpose are not reaching their full potential and often face a variety of internal struggles as well. These struggles might include feelings of inadequacy, a lack of motivation, and a pervasive sense of dissatisfaction that colors every aspect of their lives. Without a clear sense of direction, they may find it challenging to make meaningful decisions or cultivate the resilience needed to overcome obstacles. This can create a cycle of frustration, where the absence of purpose leads to inaction, and inaction reinforces the belief that growth and success are unattainable. Purpose provides the foundation for self-confidence, perseverance, and fulfillment— qualities that transform life from mere existence into something truly meaningful.

During my tenure in retail as an assistant store manager for Kmart, I had a very close encounter with a colleague who lived without purpose. I was transferred from

Bemidji, Minnesota, to the Minneapolis/St. Paul market. The store manager at this location had been with the company for many years. Due to their consistent performance, they were granted the privilege of remaining permanently at this store without being transferred. My initial impression was neutral. I figured they must be doing something right for the store's performance, otherwise, they wouldn't have had their "no transfer" request honored as being transferred was a non-negotiable part of the job.

I soon learned, however, that this individual was terribly unhappy as a store manager, was not fulfilled by their career path, and clearly was not living a life on purpose. I began to notice some things, like the hurtful, cutting comments about other members of the store's leadership team and a very disengaged attitude toward the store and its daily operations. In particular, they seemed to almost enjoy making the work life of their team members, especially the merchandise manager, miserable.

This individual also seemed to go out of their way to make vacation requests and any other time-off requests seem like a really big problem for them—going so far as to require team members to sacrifice our days off, strongly implying that it was our act of penance for receiving time off. Anyone who has ever worked retail learns almost immediately that the single biggest challenge in a retail career path is the sheer number of hours required for the successful operation of a store.

As an assistant store manager, you're working when everyone else is off, especially during the holidays. We were required to work a minimum of forty-eight hours per week. After the Christmas chaos one year, having kept track of all my extra hours worked at no additional compensation (we were on salary), I sat down and determined that I was making $1.77 per hour—I almost quit on the spot!

Looking back, I've realized this individual's behavior was a textbook example of the adage "hurting people, hurt people." They were miserable, so they wanted everyone else around them to be miserable too. At the company's annual family picnic that summer, the personnel manager asked me to bring my guitar to sing some songs for the kids. While I was performing, the store manager—who had clearly had more than their fair share of adult beverages—came up to me, lightly slapped my face a couple of times, and made fun of the song I was singing in front of the children. The thought of slapping them back crossed my mind, but I knew that would only make a bad situation even worse, especially given the poor example the kids had just witnessed.

I worked with this individual for approximately one year before I was transferred to what would be my final store during my assistant manager tenure. There were two things I resolved as a result: First, I would never treat people the way they did. Second, I would never trade my purpose in life for the security of a position or income—no matter the cost. Being stuck in such a position would never allow me to keep growing and moving forward. Reflecting on our past often helps us realize that the people we've encountered can teach us what NOT to do as much as what to do.

Think about people whose lives you do not want to emulate. What types of characteristics do they possess? What are their habits or lifestyle choices? Write your answers below:

- _____
  _____

- _____
  _____

- _____
  _____

Now think about people whom you admire. What about their lives inspires you?

- _____

  _____

- _____

  _____

- _____

  _____

In the next chapter, we'll explore how to discover your purpose. As you see above, I've included space for you to jot down answers, ideas, and reflections throughout the book. Are you ready? Let's dive in!

If you need more space to write or journal on any of the questions or prompts, there's a NOTES page provided at the end of each chapter.

> "PURPOSE IN LIFE IS FAR MORE IMPORTANT THAN PROPERTY OR POSSESSIONS. HAVING MORE TO LIVE WITH IS NO SUBSTITUTE FOR HAVING MORE TO LIVE FOR."
> — Nicky Gumbel

NOTES

_____

_____

_____

_____

_____

_____

_____

_____

_____

_____

CHAPTER 2

FINDING YOUR PURPOSE

In this chapter, we'll give you a toolkit that will come in handy as we help you discover your purpose. We'll also identify your strengths, explore your passions, and pinpoint the things that truly matter to you, such as your values. Along the way, I'll share personal stories to illustrate how I used these same tools to find my own purpose.

In my time on this beautiful planet, I've tried many different things, succeeding in some and failing in others. I've dabbled in building models, launching Estes rockets, and amateur inventing—I even participated in the local 4-H club (I won a blue ribbon for a rocket launcher I built and entered in the fair). I also tried archery and little league baseball, though I wasn't very good—I had no arm, couldn't catch well, and was only an average hitter. Football wasn't my strength either. While I was fast, running up and down the field while suited up made me feel like I was just rattling around in the gear—I was far too skinny for the sport.

For jobs and career paths, I've sold Christmas cards door to door, delivered newspapers, cut lawns, worked as a restaurant busboy and dishwasher, and then moved into my position as a stock boy in the personal care department (healthy and beauty aids in my day) at Kmart. This led to my first professional career experience as an assistant store manager. When I left that industry after close to a decade, I began my B2B (business-to-business) selling career. I sold copiers for Monroe Systems for Business, mailing equipment for Frieden Alcatel, and programs for Dale Carnegie, which led me to my current industry of office furniture sales.

Looking back on these varied experiences, with careful reflection, I see how each one shaped my journey of discovering my true purpose. Based on my experience, I have compiled a step-by-step process that will allow you to find your purpose. While it is laid out linearly, you may hop back and forth throughout your process because, as we all know, life moves in many different directions.

WII-FM, or "What's In It For Me," is often considered the most popular radio station on the planet, and the truth is, we all have our own personal station. It plays constantly in the background of our lives, influencing much of what motivates us. So, how does developing your purpose tie into what's in it for you? While it may sound contradictory to say that WII-FM is both the most popular station and uniquely personal to each of us, the reality is that each person's motivations and desires are tuned to their own station, yet we all listen to the same frequency—what benefits us personally.

STEP 1: IDENTIFY YOUR INTERESTS

Identifying your interests is a simple first step in uncovering your purpose. Some may find it harder than others, but press on—you'll get there. For me, as mentioned in the introduction, my interests include music, travel, golf, pickleball, tennis, walking, following super motocross racing, following my favorite sports teams, and reading on various subjects. I'm also passionate about personal and professional growth, as well as speaking to and uplifting others.

We all have things we excel at—playing an instrument, singing, writing, athletics, coaching and mentoring, photography, science, mathematics, listening well to others, telling stories, organizing, leading, being a good parent, or simply getting things done. These abilities are not just hobbies or skills; they are often clues to our deeper purpose. When we identify and hone those strengths, we align ourselves with what we are naturally drawn to do, allowing us to contribute meaningfully to the world around us.

As an example, my wife's hair stylist, Lori, doesn't just do hair—she's someone who truly listens to what her clients have to say, sharing in their human experience. Tamela's sister referred Tamela to Lori, and now all of my girls—including my granddaughter—get their hair cuts from Lori. She's like a part of our family and knows as much or more about our family as anyone. She listens, asks questions, and genuinely cares about those who sit in her chair. She is a people lifter and her focus (demonstrated by the arrows) is constantly facing out toward others.

OTHERS-FOCUSED

My mother-in-law–Grandma June as we all lovingly call her–is in her early nineties, still drives, and lives on her own. About five years ago it looked like she may start to need a walker. Tamela mentioned this in passing to Lori, saying that we were looking to buy one. Lori stopped her. "I have one that's no longer being used. Let me bring it to your next cut and she can have it." We tried to give her something for it, but she wouldn't hear of it.

Lori is constantly doing things like this for all of her clients, and it's one of the many reasons they go to only her for their hair—though it doesn't hurt that she is really good at cutting hair, too. So while Lori's title is hair stylist, her purpose is much more than that. Her job is simply the vehicle that allows her to carry out her unique purpose.

Another one of my others-focused hometown heroes is my brother-in-law, Michael Doughty, who's had a major impact on my life. We first met when his family moved into our neighborhood in my early teens. He introduced me to motocross racing and mentored me in every aspect of the sport. His father was a retired lieutenant colonel in the U.S. Air Force, and as a family, they had lived all over the world while serving our country.

Michael has had a very successful career with Yamaha Motor Corporation's Motorsports Division, and he and my sister Tamara have moved all over the country during his tenure. One thing they've been consistent with across all these moves is this: wherever they end up, they form lifelong friendships with others. My older sister Tamara is a big part of that too, as they both have huge hearts and are always going out of their way to help others. It's just how they roll.

My parents sort of followed them around as they moved from place to place as my dad hated the cold weather here in the midwest. When Mom and Dad moved into the winter of their lives, Michael and Tamara moved them in with the family, and even now, my sister remains my mother's primary caregiver. This is a huge sacrifice they both willingly made and one that will reap heavenly rewards; both of them are true servant leaders.

Almost every time Tamela and I visit them in Canton, Georgia, somebody else has just left. We jokingly refer to their home as the Doughty B&B. So many people come through that you need to make sure you check in with the hosts to see if your week is still available.

Some years ago, I was at a SuperCross event in Dallas, Texas, with Michael, in a suite at the Dallas Cowboys stadium. I overheard Michael share his story with another Yamaha employee. Surprisingly, for as long as I've known him, I'd never heard his story before.

He said that as a youngster while riding motorcycles out in the desert, a guy pulled up to where they were riding in a really cool van, unloaded Yamaha motorcycles, and said he worked for Yamaha. I can't recall the exact title of the guy, but Michael said at that very moment, he identified what he wanted to do. "I want to do what this guy is doing," he said. "To me, it looks like he's selling fun!"

Michael moved out to California right after he was done with high school and everything he did, from working at a Yamaha dealer to selling cars and B2B insurance was done as building blocks to ultimately go to work for Yamaha. He started as regional manager and held almost every position imaginable, including running their snowmobile division and race team while living in Minnesota.

He's a favorite among Yamaha dealer owners as he understands the world they live in better than most, and his current position is General Manager of motorcycles, running motorcycles for all of North America. He's a true example of someone who identified his purpose early in life and never wavered in their pursuit of it. He's also extremely generous to all and my supplier for almost all of my Yamaha gear. I'm a really great brand ambassador for Yamaha, too! Thank you, Michael, for living a life well-lived, on purpose.

PROMPT: IDENTIFY YOUR INTERESTS

What did you love doing as a child, and how might that connect to your passions today?

- _____

- _____

- _____

- _____

- _____

What activities make you lose track of time because you enjoy them so much? Write your responses below:

- _____

- _____

- _____

What type of work or activity would you gladly do for free?

- _____

- _____

- _____

STEP 2: IDENTIFY YOUR STRENGTHS

Whether it's an innate trait or a skill you've developed, identifying your strengths helps you align with areas that support your purpose.

PROMPT: IDENTIFY YOUR STRENGTHS

What skills or talents come naturally to you, and how do you feel when you use them?

- _____

- _____

- _____

- _____

- _____

Describe a time when you felt proud of something you accomplished. What skills or strengths did you use?

_____

_____

_____

_____

_____

STEP 3: CONSIDER YOUR DISLIKES

Just as discovering passions can shape our interests, recognizing what we don't enjoy is equally important in understanding ourselves better. By acknowledging the activities, environments, or behaviors that drain our energy or leave us unfulfilled, we can be more intentional to focus on pursuits that align with our values and talents. Dislikes act as guideposts, steering us away from distractions and helping us identify what truly matters.

For example, you'll never see me jumping out of a perfectly good airplane. I have absolutely no interest in experiencing the sheer adrenaline rush involved in such an activity. Similarly, many people may not thrive in overly competitive environments because they dislike the pressure.

Some people may discover they dislike repetitive, detail-heavy tasks like bookkeeping or data entry. While these are valuable skills, not everyone finds joy in precision work—and that's okay. Others may feel themselves drained by excessive social interactions, preferring more solitude to recharge and reflect. Recognizing what you dislike doesn't discount the importance of those activities; rather, it allows you to move closer to aligning yourself with your purpose.

PROMPT: CONSIDER YOUR DISLIKES

What are some things that you dread doing? What about that task do you dislike? Is it the environment? The people it entails? The task itself? Write your reflections below.

- _____

- _____

- _____

- _____

STEP 4: ASSESS YOUR VALUES

Assessing your values is a foundational step in discovering your purpose because your values represent what truly matters to you. They act as a compass, guiding your decisions and helping you live a life that feels authentic and meaningful.

If I asked you "Who are you?" how would you respond? Most people would offer a string of titles or labels that give them a sense of who they are. Those labels can give us a lot of insight as to what we prioritize and value in our lives. When I asked myself "Who am I?" in preparation for writing this book, I came up with the following list:

- First, I am a Christian.
- I am a citizen of the United States of America.
- I am a husband, father, grandfather, and friend.
- Last, I am a sales professional, author, speaker, musician, mentor, and coach.

As a person of strong faith, it is a no-brainer to list Christian first in my list—because, truthfully, it's Whose I am, and I would be nothing without my Lord and Savior. (Please see the invitation at the very end of this book for more information on Whose you are.) I also love and appreciate my country and the freedoms that it ensures, strongly value my family, and have had a varied and fulfilling career. All of these are things I value in my life and have shaped me into the person I am today.

What you write down depends on what you find valuable—maybe you included something about your ethnicity or your family's rich cultural traditions. Or perhaps you wrote down your place in your family's birth order, such as "baby of the family," or "eldest child" because you strongly relate to the characteristics commonly possessed by one of these positions. All of these can illuminate what really matters to you and how that influences how you see yourself.

PROMPT: ASSESS YOUR VALUES

When you consider who you are, what identifiers come to mind?

- _____

- _____

- _____

- _____

- _____

STEP 5: EXAMINE YOUR EXPERIENCES

Examining your experiences can help you notice patterns, challenges and accomplishments, which can show you when you are acting either in or out of line with your purpose. I am confident that reflection and examination will prove to be one of the greatest tools in finding your true purpose. It surely has been one of the most important for me.

Racing motocross proved to be a seminal experience for me as it taught me I could do things I was initially very uncomfortable doing. I was hesitant to start but stuck with it, got better and grew to love it. It also brought discipline and a new level of physical fitness into my life as it's a very physically demanding sport. With the confidence I gained from that experience, I began to see myself accomplishing more and willing to try more new things. It also led me to see myself as a motorcycle mechanic in the motocross industry and formed the basis for my plan to attend technical school in Eau Claire to do exactly that. However, as you will see, my plans definitely changed.

Another growing interest for me was music. As a little boy of five without headphones, I would sit with my ear to the speaker of my parent's council-sized stereo and sing along with the songs of the musical group The Monkeys. I would sing at the top of my lungs so I could hear myself and, like both my parents, I guess I had a pretty good voice. I sang all the time and loved to listen to music. Then, I signed up for choir in junior high and tried out for every solo that came up—and got most of them.

At the same time, my older sister got a guitar, took some lessons, and started singing and playing at church. I figured if she could play the guitar, so could I. I didn't officially pick up the guitar just then, but every now and then, I'd sneak into my sister's room when she wasn't around, pull her guitar out from under her bed, and mess around, trying to get a good sound out of it. Now, fast forward to age fifteen. Somehow, while messing around on her guitar, I stumbled across a G chord, and out came this rich, beautiful sound that resonated through my whole body... I was hooked!

At that age, I had started to earn money from my first jobs and began building an album collection (yup, albums and 8-track tapes were all we had back then). Someone introduced me to a new singer/songwriter named Dan Fogelberg, whose many hits were rising on the charts. I also bought my 1st acoustic guitar and became completely immersed in trying to learn his music and, specifically, his style of playing the acoustic guitar, which was with his fingers instead of a pick. I worked at it day and night with every spare moment I had. I'd play till my fingers bled from pushing on the strings, and I practiced the same songs over and over to the point of driving everyone else in the house bananas. But I was getting better, and with my ability to sing, I was actually getting pretty good.

In my late teens, I started to think I could perform as a solo acoustic coffee house musician. Then, I got to see Fogelberg in concert in Madison, Wisconsin, my senior year, in a solo acoustic performance—and I convinced myself that was something I could do. He was absolutely amazing as a solo acoustic performer; I suspect some of you reading this book may have seen him perform solo as well and wholeheartedly agree!

Considering the nature of my dream, it should be no surprise what my closest friends and mom told me. (My mom loved my voice but told me I'd never be good enough on the guitar; of course, I believe she was just looking out for me.) The message consistently was "No way, you're not good enough," "What makes you think you could do that," etc. That kind of feedback only made me more determined to succeed and revealed to me how determined I could be. I learned that the best way to get me to do something was to tell me it couldn't be done.

As the photo below shows, I became a headliner in the local Eau Claire, Wisconsin, market and played regularly at Houligans, Howard Johnson's pub, and many other regional locations. I also began singing at weddings, sometimes doing two per Saturday. It was a really fun time—I was making some OK money, picking up some momentum, but most importantly, learning to believe in myself, which set the foundation for me to identify my lifelong purpose. The determination I developed at this time has served me very well in my adult life.

Me as a headliner at a local Eau Claire, Wisconsin, pub. (Love the 'do, don't you?)

And finally I hadn't planned for college at all; instead, as previously mentioned, tech school was the plan to put me on track as a motorcycle mechanic. I mean, what else would you want to do with your life at eighteen? However, at my final senior choir concert, I sang a solo and was approached after the concert by the concert choir director of the University of Wisconsin, Eau Claire, Morris D. Hayes. He said to me, "Mitchell, you have a very developed high tenor voice for someone your age. If you'll come and sing in my choir, I will pay for your first full year of college."

It was an offer I couldn't refuse. After discussing it with my parents, I realized that the only thing better than college was free college. When asked what my major would be, I responded "Music, of course!" And, as God is my witness, I thought I'd sit around listening to albums all day and learn how to sing and play songs that I wanted to add to my coffee house gig setlist. I honestly had NO idea that there was an organized, very rigorous curriculum around the study of music.

Why didn't this occur to me? Because my musical gift was auditory. What does that mean in English? I learned to play the guitar and how to sing—and still do, by the way—by listening. I didn't know it then, but I am sure of it now: My heavenly Father gave this gift to me. I can see the chords on my guitar in my mind when I'm listening to the music. Not all chords but most of the basic ones, and I can hear where the music wants to go as I play it. It's a gift I treasure.

Now, back to my story. You might imagine my surprise when I showed up for my orientation, thinking I'd be signing a few forms and learning what time choir practice was, when they hit me with questions like "Where's your accompanist for your vocal performance audition?" "What level of music theory training have you had?" "How proficient are you on the piano?" "What's your music composition background?" "How many instruments do you play?" (Apparently, being a singer/songwriter on acoustic guitar wasn't big in the Renaissance era.)

Needless to say, I was completely unprepared, overwhelmed, and a bit angry. I didn't sign up for all that! I just wanted to sing in choir and play my kind of music. Once the shock wore off and I understood what I had signed on for, I figured that I'd at least learn something that would help me if the coffee house thing really took off.

One of my very first music courses was basic music theory, which I have come to learn is the mathematical study of music—why it sounds the way it does, how to write and work with it, and the various reasons that it moves and sounds the way it does. It's fascinating, really. However, one other small barrier to entry for me was that I didn't, and still don't, read music. (But then again, neither does James Taylor.) I could identify and understand chord symbols for the guitar, but picking out a note on a page and playing that on the guitar or piano was a no-go.

"I FIND THAT AS I WRITE, IT'S A SORT OF PROCESS
THAT'S OUT OF MY CONTROL. IT'S OFTEN AS
THOUGH RATHER THAN WRITING THE SONGS, I'M
JUST THE FIRST PERSON TO HEAR THEM."

— James Taylor

There I was on day one, walking into my first music theory class. I knew I was dead as soon as I walked in because they had the musical staff permanently plumbed into the blackboards. (We didn't have erasable whiteboards or the kind of AV you find in most classrooms today.) Enter Dr. Dave Baker, who launches into his lesson. I surprised myself by actually keeping up—until he shifted into a discussion of the bass clef, which is the arrangement of the notes on the staff that caters to the lower-voiced instruments in, say, an orchestra.

I was struggling to remember the acronym for bass clef. In a panic, I leaned over to the girl sitting next to me and said, "I know it's Every Good Boy Does Fine for the lines and FACE for the spaces in treble clef, but what's the acronyms for bass clef?" She gave me a puzzled look and replied "You don't know how to read music?" I told her no, to which she asked, "Well, what are you doing in the class?" I said, "They told me I had to take it." That girl just happened to be my now-wife, Tamela Sue Federwitz Larson!

In order to effectively discover your purpose, it is crucial to examine where your life choices have taken you. Upon doing so, you will clearly see the fingerprints of God. What if Morris Hayes hadn't been at my last concert? I might never have gone to college, taken music theory, or grown my confidence as a musician. College provided me with the tools to communicate effectively and feel comfortable performing for an audience, which opened the door to many future gigs. I also might never have met my amazing wife—my best friend, the mother of our two wonderful children—or written this book. That single encounter with Hayes completely changed the direction of my life.

PROMPT: EXAMINE YOUR EXPERIENCES

What are some significant moments in your life and why do they stand out?

- _____

- _____

- _____

- _____

- _____

Think of a time when you felt truly fulfilled. Who were you with and what were you doing?

- _____

- _____

- _____

What experiences have shaped your values and beliefs most?

- _____

- _____

- _____

Now that you've taken the five steps to find your purpose, it is time to draft your purpose statement. Use concise and clear language to summarize your purpose. A strong purpose statement typically includes:

- **What you do:** Your actions or contributions.
- **Why you do it:** The deeper motivation or impact.
- **Who benefits:** The audience or cause you aim to serve.

For example:
- "I empower individuals to embrace their authentic selves and unlock their potential so they can live fulfilling lives."
- "I use my creativity and storytelling skills to empower communities and inspire positive change."

Your purpose statement:

_____

_____

_____

_____

In the next chapter, we'll take a deep dive into the exciting process of developing your purpose. While uncovering your purpose begins with self-discovery—reflecting on your values, passions, strengths, and life experiences—bringing it to life requires intentional action. This chapter will guide you through practical steps to refine your vision, set meaningful goals, and align your daily choices with what truly matters to you.

"SUCCESS IS THE PROGRESSIVE REALIZATION
OF A WORTHWHILE DREAM OR GOAL, IN ALIGNMENT
WITH YOUR PURPOSE."
—Mitch Larson

NOTES

CHAPTER 3

DEVELOPING YOUR PURPOSE

Once you've identified your purpose, how do you go about developing it? It's important to remember that personal and professional growth takes time and occurs in small steps. Whenever my girls run into a challenge, I remind them of this truth all the time: You can never climb a mountain in one day, but if you take a step or two up the mountain every day, you'll reach the top sooner than you think. Nothing that I'm recommending in this chapter is complex; they're all very basic, simple adjustments that anyone is capable of doing.

COMPONENTS OF YOUR PURPOSE-DEVELOPMENT PROCESS

- Stretch your comfort zone
- Seek mentorship
- Develop discipline
- Harness the power of habit
- Examine your habit structure
- The importance of personal responsibility
- Persistence with purpose

Let's examine each of these steps.

STRETCH YOUR COMFORT ZONE

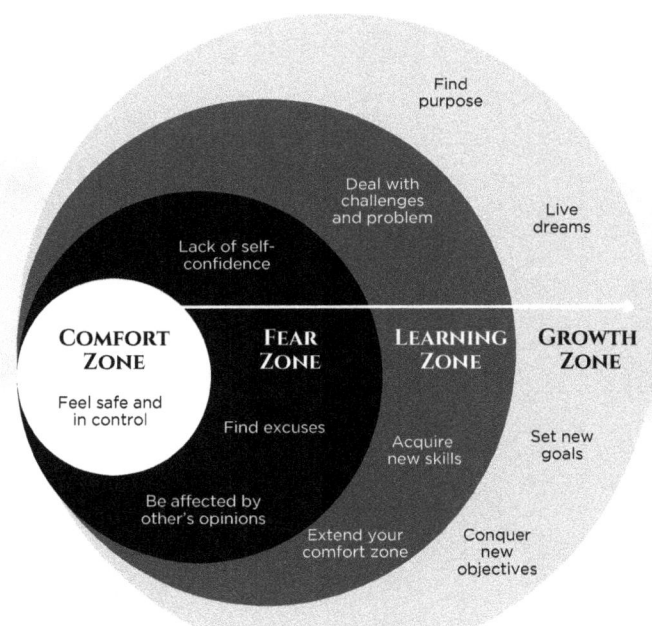

THE COMFORT ZONE - A KEY TOOL IN ANYONE'S GROWTH AND DEVELOPMENT

The previous diagram is a visual representation of why the thought process and experience behind pushing the edges of your comfort zone is not only critical to finding your purpose but absolutely essential in anyone's ongoing growth as an individual.

The concept is a rather simple one. Imagine taking a rubber band and stretching it, then letting it return to its natural state. It's true that the growth that occurred from that single stretch may be almost completely imperceptible, but if the process is repeated, on purpose, over and over, the end result for the rubber band or the change you see in your abilities, can be astonishing. I have personally witnessed this growth in myself and countless others because we stayed committed to the process of stretching ourselves.

On the flip side, I have also observed that if we don't purposefully push ourselves out of our comfort zones and live closer to the "fringes of fear" as I know it, we limit our growth and create situations that are highly conducive to opening one's mouth, inserting a thumb, and becoming a victim.

Pushing past your comfort zone allows you to discover or deepen your purpose because it forces you to confront your fears, limitations, and untapped potential. Growth rarely happens in comfort; by stepping into the unknown, you gain new perspectives, develop resilience, and uncover abilities or passions you may not have realized you had.

When I sold enrollments to the various Dale Carnegie programs, I used the example of stretching one's comfort zone, as people clearly identified with it and it helped prospective enrollees understand how their participation in one of our programs would result in them accomplishing their objective.

Whether they wanted to improve their speaking abilities, enhance their sales skills, become better presenters, or grow as stronger leaders, once they understood the process and how necessary changes could occur over time to achieve their desired results, they approached the experience with an improved attitude, greater confidence, and increased hope for a positive outcome.

Motocross racing was a hobby of mine that taught me invaluable lessons about the importance of pushing myself beyond my comfort zone. Whether it was confronting my fear of the motorcycle's power or attempting to navigate challenging tracks far beyond my skill level, each experience pushed me to grow in ways I didn't anticipate. I learned that stepping into discomfort is often the key to unlocking hidden potential. Even when I failed or felt out of my depth, the process built resilience, adaptability, and a deeper understanding of my own capabilities. These lessons extend far beyond motocross and have become a guiding principle in my pursuit of purpose and growth.

PROMPT: STRETCH YOUR COMFORT ZONE

What activities, environments, or situations make you feel most comfortable and secure? Why?

- _____

- _____

- _____

- _____

When was the last time you stepped outside your comfort zone? What did you learn from the experience?

- _____

- _____

- _____

- _____

How does staying in your comfort zone align (or not align) with your goals and values?

- _____

- _____

- _____

- _____

In what ways might expanding your comfort zone help you discover or deepen your purpose?

- _____

- _____

- _____

- _____

If you viewed challenges as opportunities for growth instead of risks to be avoided, how might your mindset shift?

- _____

- _____

- _____

- _____

Seek Mentorship

I was fortunate to understand the value of mentors, coaches, and leaders early in my life. Maybe it's because I knew inherently that I didn't really know anything. Whatever the reason, it always made sense to me that if I was going to try and do something, I ought to find someone who's already doing it, observe them and if they are proficient and willing, ask them to answer your questions and show you what to do.

As previously mentioned, Kmart was one of my earliest jobs, and during my tenure there, I worked closely with a department manager who taught me how to properly merchandise and stock an area. More importantly, he showed me the value of making lists, a habit I would carry with me to this very day.

Side note here: In 1890, Frederick Taylor, an aspiring business consultant of the time, met Andrew Carnegie, industrialist and head of Carnegie Steel, at a cocktail party in Pittsburg, Pennsylvania. Carnegie challenged Taylor to give him some good advice about management and promised that if the advice was any good, he'd pay him $10,000 for it. Taylor accepted the challenge and then taught Carnegie how to make a list. "List the top ten most important things you can do and begin to take action on them, starting with number one," Taylor advised. Did the advice work, you ask? A week later, Taylor received a check for $10,000, the equivalent of $280,000 in today's dollars.

Mentorship also played a crucial role in our success as Tamela and I actively built a direct-selling business which we continue to support, and we both deeply value the profound impact it has had on our lives. One benefit of our specific business was the access we had to their personal and professional development system. The only way we can describe this resource—the books, audiotapes, seminars, speakers, and systematic methods to grow and develop the individual—was "invaluable!" We both believe that the success we achieved during our time building our business has had a greater impact on our lives than any other endeavor we have ever pursued, in part because of the training provided to us.

Not only did we learn basic business skills like records keeping, organizational skills, time and calendar management, and scheduling but it introduced us to a whole new way of thinking and positive mental attitudes. As an organization, we followed a regular monthly reading program that included some leadership classics like Dale Carnegie's How to Win Friends and Influence People and How to Stop Worrying and Start Living, as well as Norman Vincent Peale's The Power of Positive Thinking; marriage staples like Gary Chapman's The Five Love Languages, Ed Cole's Communication, Sex, & Money, He Said, She Said by Deborah Tannen, and Man of Steel and Velvet by Aubrey Andelin; and money management titles like The Richest Man in Babylon by George S. Clason, and Rich Dad, Poor Dad by Robert Kiyosaki—among so many other titles that set out to teach readers strategies for life.

Perhaps the most transformative mentoring I had early on in my career was the Dale Carnegie Training. This experience exposed me to a systematic program that helps people grow and develop using a method that stretches their comfort zones on a weekly basis. The key to the Carnegie programs is their length. For example, their public speaking and sales course are twelve weeks long, and their management seminar is six weeks long. The result of these longer programs is multifold. Personally, when I took the public speaking program, it was more comfortable to make subtle changes on a weekly basis over a longer period of time compared with rushing all the changes in a short period of time. This pace allowed the changes to become a part of my habit structure and thus stick. The program length, along with opportunities to conduct both orientations and a variety of value-added workshops, really helped me hone my ability to speak in front of a group and equipped me with the skill set to fine-tune my storytelling and messaging.

Interestingly enough, my time with Dale Carnegie training led me to my job at Herman Miller. When Tamela and I moved to Minneapolis/St. Paul from Bemidji Minnesota, for a Kmart transfer, our cost of living tripled overnight and it became necessary for her to find work ASAP. She worked with a temporary employment agency, and after a few temporary jobs, she was hired as a collections specialist at a new office furniture dealership in Edina, Minnesota, called Facility Systems, Inc. They were the new Herman Miller office furniture dealer in Minneapolis/St. Paul at an explosive time for the office furniture industry, which was growing in leaps and bounds.

While Tamela thoroughly enjoyed the company culture and all of the people she worked with, the pressure of collections and constantly calling people and asking them why they weren't paying their bills was very stressful, and it started taking a toll on her health. She approached the owners and asked for a position change to something less stressful. Because she had proven herself already, they moved her into an admin position of invoice coordinator, a position she held for more than ten years until she retired when we adopted our first daughter.

Because of Tamela's job, I got to know all of the people at both the dealer, FSI, and manufacturer, Herman Miller, including the new regional manager Jerry Erickson. Funnily enough, while working for Dale Carnegie, we bumped into each other at a local car wash not long after their company Christmas party. As we conversed, Erickson asked what I was doing for work, and I told him about Dale Carnegie's programs. He noted that he'd heard very good things about the programs and encouraged me to come and see him sometime soon.

He gave me his card at the car wash and I called him the very next Monday. I ended up leaving him a voicemail, a very common way of setting appointments back then. What I didn't know was that Jerry's world was completely insane because the industry was exploding. He'd been key in the growth and development of the people on his team, and a number of them had just accepted promotions and he was trying to backfill their positions. So, it took six months of calling him once a week on Monday morning, the time I set aside in my schedule to follow up with potential clients, and leaving a politely persistent voicemail before he returned my call.

I ended up enrolling (selling) three of his team members into our management program, and as a value add, we did a sales workshop for Jerry's entire team. When he was introducing my sales manager, Mark, and me, he told his team that I was the most persistent salesperson he had ever experienced in his career. I didn't know at that time that Jerry wasn't one to dole out compliments easily, and I learned later that if he said something, he really meant it. Mark commented after the workshop that it was a really special thing for him to say and that it obviously lent credibility to our session.

Fast forward about eighteen months and I found myself in transition from Dale Carnegie because the Gulf War had broken out and my single largest account at the time, Northwest Airlines, suspended all non-essential expenditures because the cost of jet fuel had literally doubled, almost tripled, overnight. I went from hero to zero overnight as well and was working an overnight shift at a Dow Chemical company assembling industrial water treatment filters, and looking for a new job during the day, running on almost NO sleep.

I was in the FSI parking lot waiting to pick up my wife from work, with my seat back, eyes closed, trying to get an extra minute or two of rest when there was a friendly knock on my window. It was Jerry Erickson. I rolled my window down,

"Mitch, how are you?" he asked.

"Fantastic, Jerry, just running a little low on sleep right now," I said.

He inquired further, and I quickly explained how the Gulf War had unexpectedly ended my time with Dale Carnegie and that I was looking for my next opportunity. He got an opportunistic look on his face before asking if I'd ever considered working for Herman Miller.

"It never crossed my mind, Jerry, but I always keep my options open."

About three months later, I was the newest member of Herman Miller's North Central region as a market manager, and while I couldn't have fully realized it at the time, I had just stepped through the door of the longest and most prosperous portion of my work life in an industry that helped me grow and develop as a professional.

Jerry's belief in my abilities, despite my lack of experience, not only opened the door to my career at Herman Miller but also highlighted the resilience and persistence that have shaped my professional journey. If Jerry hadn't had the experience of me calling on him as a customer first, I never would have gone to work for Herman Miller. I had no experience in the industry, but Jerry knew I could sell, and he could teach me the furniture part. What he saw in me was my resilient attitude and persistence. These two qualities are what I have built on and leveraged my entire working life. Also worth mentioning is that because he believed in me, I found it easier to believe in myself.

PROMPT: SEEK MENTORSHIP

What qualities do you look for in a mentor? How do these qualities align with your values and your goals for personal growth?

- _____

- _____

- _____

- _____

If you could find a mentor right now, what area of your life would you want their guidance in? Why is this area important to your purpose?

- _____

- _____

- _____

- _____

What steps can you take today to seek out a mentor who aligns with your values and purpose?

- _____

- _____

- _____

- _____

THE ROLE OF DISCIPLINE

Discipline is the cornerstone of success, driving you to take action when it's difficult and preventing you from engaging in harmful behaviors. You can't accomplish anything without discipline. Discipline is the act of making yourself do something when you don't feel like it (i.e., exercising, writing, studying, or working), but it also acts as a barrier that keeps you from doing something when you shouldn't (i.e., eating too much or the wrong things, playing when you should be working, watching or reading the wrong things). Another way of saying that is you have to be on purpose with your thinking and properly manage your thoughts.

For example, my journey through racing motocross taught me the value of discipline because to participate in racing at all, I had to get my first job to support the costs of motorcycle maintenance, repair, modification, and fuel. Entry fees, equipment and riding gear, supplies, and food money also needed to be paid for.

Then, to take it a step further, it took discipline to train on my own to develop the necessary stamina, endurance, and conditioning required for racing well. This training involved running, focused weight training, stretching, and other activities. On top of my training, I had to learn to manage my schedule between school, work, and other activities to find the time to practice and prepare for the next race. Naturally, I loved every second of it all, but realistically, it was just what you had to do in order to race motocross.

I see this whole experience as a foundational moment in my life that allowed me to develop the necessary discipline and habit structure to succeed in any endeavor. At that time in my life, racing motocross was a definite purpose, and all of the above were the ingredients necessary for turning that purpose into a reality in my life.

PROMPT: THE ROLE OF DISCIPLINE

In what areas of your life do you feel the most disciplined? What routines or habits have helped you maintain discipline in these areas?

* _____

* _____

* _____

In which areas do you struggle to practice discipline? What challenges or obstacles prevent you from staying consistent?

* _____

* _____

* _____

Think of a time when practicing discipline led to a positive outcome. What was the result, and how did it feel to stay disciplined through that process?

- _____

- _____

- _____

What small, incremental steps can you take to start practicing more discipline in one area of your life?

- _____

- _____

- _____

THE POWER OF HABIT

Are your habits serving you and helping you move forward or are they hurting you? Building a strong habit structure is one of the foundational elements of achieving sustainable success in life.

The reason I want to discuss habits right after discipline is because discipline is a primary ingredient in forming effective habits. If we engage discipline on the front end of any change we want to make in our lives, we will quickly see it's one of the primary ingredients to forming effective habits. Once anything you do becomes a habit, you no longer have to think about it or work at doing it. Discipline has done its duty.

Habits can be helpful or harmful. I lost over thirty-three pounds between September and October of last year but gained at least half of that weight back over the course of six months. I had started a new eating program that produced weight loss, but after a while, I went back to eating and drinking exactly what I had been before I started my weight loss program. Is this a helpful or harmful habit? Harmful, of course. I restarted the eating program that produced the weight loss and have lost another twelve pounds. What do I need to change and make a habit of to avoid regaining the weight? I need to manage my post-program eating and exercise.

In an excerpt from John C. Maxwell's Thinking for a Change, a quote he came across years ago described habit like this:

> I am your constant companion. I am your greatest helper or heaviest burden. I will push you onward or drag you down to failure, I am completely at your command. Half of the things you do you might just as well turn over to me and I will be able to do them quickly and correctly. I am easily managed - you must merely be firm with me. Show me exactly how you want it done and after a few lessons, I will do it automatically. I am the servant of all great people; and alas of all failures as well. Those who are great, I have made great, Those who are failures, I have made failures. I am not a machine, though I work with the precision of a machine plus the intelligence of a person. You may run me for profit or run me for ruin - it makes no difference to me. Take me, train me, be firm with me (discipline) and I will place the world at your feet. Be easy with me and I will destroy you. Who am I? I am habit!

This is the most accurate and profound piece I have ever seen on the importance of a good habit structure. Maxwell has said that he can spend a day with someone and quickly determine whether they will identify and achieve their purpose in life based on observing how and what they do with their time. The secret of anyone's success, yours and mine, is hidden in our daily habit structure.

"DEVELOPING A GOOD HABIT STRUCTURE IS ONE OF
THE KEYS TO ALL SUSTAINABLE SUCCESS IN LIFE."
— Mitch Larson

As discussed in The Power of Habit by Charles Duhigg, small changes lead to big differences. For example, Duhigg notes that saving $8 per day adds up to $2,920 per year. Reading just twenty pages per day can result in finishing around thirty books in a year. Walking 10,000 steps daily amounts to the equivalent of completing approximately seventy marathons over time. Small habits should never be underestimated.

PROMPT: THE POWER OF HABIT

What habits do I currently have that are serving me well in reaching my goals?

- _____

- _____

- _____

- _____

Are there any habits I've developed that are holding me back from becoming the person I want to be?

- _____

- _____

- _____

How do my habits impact my physical, mental, and emotional well-being?

- _____

- _____

- _____

- _____

What habit would I like to create to bring me closer to my ideal self?

- _____

- _____

- _____

- _____

THE IMPORTANCE OF PERSONAL RESPONSIBILITY

Mark Norman is someone who became a friend and mentor in my early professional life. He is the textbook definition of a people lifter and one of the most gifted speakers and communicators I have ever met. There is a story he often shares about growing up and how, whenever he complained about someone or something, his dad would always ask him, "Well, Mark, what are you going to do about it?" He hated hearing that question because he wanted his dad to solve his problems. However, now, as a parent, he understands and does the same thing with his children. Like Mark, it teaches them to have a problem-solving mindset instead of relying on or, even worse, expecting someone to do it for them.

Personal responsibility means you take ownership of yourself and your actions. It may not be obvious at first, but eventually, it leads to the realization that we are fully responsible for ourselves and our situation in life. The good, the bad and the ugly.

So, if at this moment we find ourselves in a really wonderful place in life filled with purpose, prosperity, great friends, and strong relationships, guess what? We most likely have the most, if not all, to do with that reality. If the total opposite of that is true, guess what? We most likely have the most, if not all, to do with that too.

As much as the national conscience doesn't want to hear this, all of us are where we are in life right now because of the decisions and choices we have made up to this point in our lives—good, bad, or ugly. If everybody is waiting for somebody to do something, nobody ends up doing anything.

If you do something for someone that they can and should do for themselves, you aren't helping them, you are hurting them and teaching them NOT to take responsibility for themselves. That thinking leads directly to the victim mentality, and when that mentality becomes a part of the national consciousness, it won't be a good day for America.

"I HAVE OBSERVED THAT SOME PEOPLE'S MINDS ARE
LIKE CEMENT, ALL MIXED UP AND PERMANENTLY SET."
— Ron Puryear

Are there any areas of your life where you may be adopting a victim mentality? How has this mindset affected your ability to move forward? What would taking responsibility look like in this situation?

- _____

- _____

- _____

- _____

PERSISTENCE WITH PURPOSE

I have chosen Thomas Edison as the key example to examine in this section because his life story is a textbook example of the value of persistence. In his eighty-four years on this planet, he showed the world that sheer determination, persistence, and talent can make a huge difference.

According to his records, Edison failed to make an electric light bulb 2,774 times—and then reached a working design. During the development of the light bulb, when asked if he had failed, he replied, "I have not failed. I've just found 10,000 ways that won't work." In relationship to that experience and process, he also said, "Just because something doesn't do what you planned it to do doesn't mean it's useless." He ended up with 1,093 patents to his name and is credited with inventing the early versions of many things we interact with in our lives on a daily basis (i.e., the telegraph, the alkaline battery, the electrographic voice recorder, the phonograph, the cinematic projector, and the list goes on).

Reflect on a time in your life when you experienced failure. How did you respond, and what did you learn from that experience?

_____

_____

_____

_____

"GENIUS IS ONE PERCENT INSPIRATION AND
NINETY-NINE PERCENT PERSPIRATION."
— Thomas Edison

NOTES

_____

_____

_____

_____

_____

_____

_____

_____

_____

CHAPTER 4

OBSTACLES TO ACCOMPLISHING YOUR PURPOSE

In this chapter, I hope to help you identify and discuss various obstacles that can and most certainly will present themselves on your journey to discovering, developing, and fulfilling your purpose.

I am no different in this regard. Like anyone else looking to do more with their life, I have encountered a large number of obstacles, including, dream stealers of every kind, cleverly disguised, because they were wearing shoes. These people included well-meaning friends, family members, teachers, loan officers at various banks, real estate agents, other sales professionals, my direct supervisors and/or organizational leaders, a variety of peers, the media, and sometimes even the current national consciousness.

While I realize this is a rather exhaustive list, whenever you try to do something new, different, or great, more often than not, you learn two things very quickly: One, you may not have as many good friends as you thought; and two, you are the most ambitious person you know.

One of the biggest and most constant obstacles we all face at some point is fear. It shows up in many different forms, but at the end of the day, it's still scary. It's important that we examine the subject of fear in-depth and also discuss how various types of fears are interrelated to the people and personalities you come in contact with on your purpose journey. It's also important that we identify ways and tools you can use to overcome and conquer your fears.

F ALSE

E VIDENCE

A PPEARING

R EAL

UNPACKING FEAR

As illustrated in the acronym above, there is hope, as I have found that "false evidence appearing real" is a very accurate descriptor of fear, and that if we unpack the reasons behind the fears that are holding us back, it's been my experience that we will almost always be able to overcome them.

Fear has been one of the greatest barriers to accomplishment in all of human history. It has robbed people of achievements, inventions, books, songs, movies, TV shows, homes, churches, and other buildings, a ton of relationships, and contributions of both social and intrinsic value of every kind. Fear has kept those ideas inside people's heads, never giving them the chance to become reality. I think we can all identify with

this, as so many of us have been "held prisoner" by our own minds and maybe still are affected by this very real human emotion at various times in our lives.

Interestingly enough, the Bible has a lot to say on the subject of fear. Here are two important verses—but there are many, many more:

- Isaiah 41:10 - "Fear not, for I am with you; be not dismayed, for I am your God; I will strengthen you, I will help you, I will uphold you with my righteous right hand."

- Joshua 1:9 - "Have I not commanded you? Be strong and courageous. Do not be frightened, and do not be dismayed, for the Lord your God is with you wherever you go."

Why is that I wonder, hmm? Could it be that the one who created us also knows what we are afraid of? I am going with a BIG yes on that one. Let's examine a few types of fears.

FEAR OF FAILURE

If I try I may not succeed; therefore, I won't try. I think this one has taken us all down at different times and certainly plays a huge part in how we examine risk, especially financial risk, associated with, say, opening your own business.

In my mid-twenties, Tamela and I thoroughly investigated a franchise opportunity that was exploding called Sounds Easy, which was out of Orem, Utah. The concept was very simple: You'd rent a space in a high-traffic area, preferably a shopping mall, bring in an inventory of the most current VHS movies (video tapes for all you youngins), and rent both the movie and the newly introduced video cassette recorders (VCR) because the cost at that moment in time made them cost prohibitive for many families. The customer would rent both for a reasonable rate. The fee structure was designed to accommodate a number of viewing options, including single video and VCR rental for one day all the way up to multiple video and VCR rentals for multiple days—and then a late fee schedule that contributed to the revenue stream.

I discovered the opportunity through the franchisee at the Paul Bunyan Mall in Bemidji, Minnesota, when I was working at the Kmart as an assistant manager. I watched his business explode, creating the need for him to double his space to accommodate the foot traffic and inventory requirements to keep up with the ever-increasing demand.

Our original business plan included franchise rights for the state of Wisconsin, with a possible option for the Minneapolis–St. Paul metro area as well. However, while we were busy shopping our business plan around to a variety of banks and potential private investors, the business model began to quickly lose momentum because the cost of the VCR was plummeting, making it easily affordable for the average American family. The franchise was on the ropes by the time we abandoned our plans and quickly went bankrupt not long after. The concept of the video rental store then exploded and sustained itself profitably for decades until its demise because of the internet and abundant content streaming availability.

Had we been successful in obtaining the necessary funding to launch the franchise, we would have surely been a failed venture with a rather painful financial death. But I shouldn't have been surprised by this franchise's downfall—my "spidey sense" was tingling often as we pursued making this business a reality. After all, I was an assistant manager at the number-one retailer on the planet (at the time), and I had a front-row seat to the astounding price drops on VCRs. My point in sharing this is that failure is not always a bad thing. Failing teaches you what not to do and provides valuable lessons and insights on corrections, preparation, and can reveal stumbling blocks that may have been missed. Those barriers just need to be identified and properly managed as a part of the pursuit of any endeavor. Many great people throughout history actually credit all of the failures they navigated through as the primary reason for their success. As long as we are learning from them and failing forward, we are moving in the right direction.

> ## "FAILURE IS NOT FATAL, BUT FAILURE TO CHANGE MIGHT BE."
> - John Wooden

FEAR OF REJECTION

This one crippled me in high school when it came to dating. I reasoned with myself: "If I ask them out they might say NO, so I won't ask." Of course, I was completely over-looking the more mature perspective that entertained the possibility that they might also say yes. Like most teens, I didn't possess that wisdom back then.

Fear of rejection also plays a large part in selling and is something that has to be overcome if you are walking the sales career path. I once heard an interesting point of view: "We're all in sales. If you're married, you performed at least one great selling job in your life." I have also found that a related barrier in this area is excuse-making.

Excuses —"Excuses are the skin of a lie, stuffed with reason." Of course, I fully understand there are legitimate reasons we all deal with, sometimes daily, that limit us, so please don't misunderstand my intent. Having said that, remember that entertaining anything less than a legitimate issue/reason will keep you from finding and fulfilling your true purpose in life.

The number one excuse people use when confronted with the possibility of trying something new is "I don't have time." Truth: We all have all the time there is! It matters how we choose to use that precious gift of time.

Here's another example from my experience. During my tenure with Kmart, it came to my attention that my next promotion was to be a transfer from Minneapolis to inner-city Chicago as a merchandise manager. A promotion in the title, maybe, but the location was a little less than desirable. (I think my internal self said, "Excuse me, but do I have 'stupid' tattooed on my forehead?"). I immediately found a job search firm, decided I wanted to give sales a shot, and ended up taking my first job in business-to-business (B2B) sales selling copiers for Monroe Systems for business back when "dirt was new" and the new business development tools we used back then were a little different than they are today.

One of the primary tools we used was the cold call. Just saying the term brings a shiver to my spine. I was instructed in my training that the key to my success was making forty (yup, you read that right) cold calls per day throughout my territory as that would provide me the proper number of leads, namely a business ready to purchase a copier, for me to hit my sales numbers and succeed in my new profession.

My first thought was, *Isn't there something else we can do to find these leads?* Why? Because I was freaking terrified of making cold calls, that's why! After my initial training, was complete and I knew more than I ever thought I could about copiers and why Monroe's was the best, it was time to pony up and go out into my territory by myself and make my very first cold call.

We had a daily check-in with our sales manager at the end of each day, so I knew I couldn't come back empty-handed. However, as I mentioned, I was nothing less than terrified to make the cold calls. Why, what if they said no? What if they were mean to me? What if they asked a question I couldn't answer? More fear of failure… I think you get the picture here. In the middle of this swirling fear, guess what my mind did to me?

Well, first, I had to swing by my house to check on the cat. Then I realized that I certainly couldn't make my first cold call on an empty stomach, could I? So, I took an unusually long lunch break that day. Then, after that, I needed to check the weather on TV because it wasn't available on our phone's weather app back then, as I didn't want to get stuck in a really bad snowstorm. (It was winter and very cold that day, well below zero. How appropriate that I was making my first "cold call" on a very cold day!) Nevertheless, when I finally ran out of good excuses, I started coming up with bad ones.

Finally, I drove into Plymouth, Minnesota, the part of my territory that was farthest north and took me the longest to get to. Then I began to search the territory for the location where this epic event would take place, and finally, after much back and forth with myself, I pulled into a business park with small office spaces, one right next to the other.

After sitting in the car for what felt like an eternity, I finally talked myself into getting out, and as God is my witness, on that freezing cold day, I discovered I had sweat through not only my shirt and suit jacket but also my overcoat. I literally had pit stains on the outside of my overcoat! However, I had decided this was the moment, so I grabbed a brochure with my business card stapled to it as I had been taught, marched myself to the first office closest to where I had parked, opened the door, allowing a blast of icy air into the small office, got a dirty look from the person behind the counter because of the cold blast, and instead of announcing who I was and why I was there like I was taught, my mind went completely blank. I vapor locked (that's when your engine simply stops working); I opened my mouth, but nothing came out, so I threw the brochure on the counter, turned around, and walked back out.

Now, with what happened next, I'm surprised they didn't call the paddy wagon and have me dragged off in a straight jacket, but right there in the parking lot, freezing my bum off, I did my very best version of a victory dance—and believe me I can't dance! My wife once asked me, "How can you play the guitar so well and can't dance?" My response? "I don't play the guitar with my feet." To me, it was a major victory. The actual call stunk and nothing came of it, sales-wise, but after I'd done it, it dawned on me that you only have to make your very first cold call—or phone call, or introduction in front of others, or group talk, insert your first here—ONE TIME! After the first one, slowly but surely, bit by bit, you get better if you don't let excuses keep you from starting.

I suspect you already know how this particular story ends. I think I made around ten calls total that first day, by the time I got there, I was much better and really not all that terrified. I was able to walk in, introduce myself, ask if they were looking at new copiers, and get a business card. I was at that job for less than a year, as it was a very high turnover industry, but by the time I left, I was blitzing multi-floor buildings, oftentimes staying one floor ahead of people trying to politely throw me out. "Didn't you see the 'NO Soliciting' signs?" The thing I was initially terrified of became one of my greatest strengths in my B2B sales career.

If I had let all of the excuses and fears keep me from at least trying to cold call, I wouldn't be here writing this book right now because I faced those types of seminal experiences, fight or flight moments, again and again throughout my entire professional career. What I've learned is that if I just keep piling these types of experiences on top of one another, I'm really learning and growing in my profession.

Now you might be saying to yourself, yeah but Mitch, well before all of this sales stuff, you were already used to singing and performing in front of people, so why was this such a big deal? Two things: First, I generally didn't have to speak much in front of audiences since I was there to sing. While the public exposure did help, singing felt like a completely different experience to me. And second, as a child, I stuttered. It wasn't a really bad one like you've perhaps heard or seen in films. In grade school, I would raise my hand, get called on, and stand up—as we often had to do back then. But when I opened my mouth to speak, nothing would come out—just like I said, vapor lock. I'd turn bright red and sit back down. And then, of course, all the uplifting positive reinforcement I got from all the other kids on the playground after they'd seen me vapor lock was particularly helpful too.

Because I've faced and overcome these issues, which required me to take radical personal responsibility and avoid excuses, I've been able to stretch my comfort zone over the years; "Just keep moving forward" is an internal self-talk mantra I developed and still use today. That mechanism was forged in the fire of events like those I've described to you. If I could do it, I believe you can too!

FEAR OF WHAT OTHERS THINK

This one is huge and never seems to go out of style. It's a persistent fear that follows us through our entire lives, personal and professional. Here are a few truths that really helped me overcome this.

Most people don't think of you as much as you think they do. Who do you spend most of your time thinking about? Yourself, your family, and things that are important and relevant to you and them. You might find that the power of observation can be very helpful here too. Are the people that you're concerned about in life where you want to be? If the answer is no, then, with all due respect, who gives a flying rip about what they think?

A very successful entrepreneur/mentor in my life once shared a story about an encounter he had with a teller at his local small-town bank. He said he was there depositing a very large check, profits from one of his businesses, and the teller started telling him why she didn't think very much of what he did for a living. His response was, "Well, thank you very much, but I don't think very much of what you think. You have a nice day."

I have one final thought to share with you on this topic. I was blessed with the ability to not care one iota what other people think of me—never have, never will. I care only what three people think about me: What do I think of me? What does my wife Tamela think of me? And, most importantly, what does my Heavenly Father think of me? That's it. Once I have those boxes checked and I know I am pursuing a good cause with a good outcome, off I go.

Yet, I recognize that people far and wide experience the fear of what others think of them. If you are someone who becomes paralyzed with this fear, I encourage you to consider this very poignant question: Are they where I want to be in life? If the answer is no, their opinion does not have value. It's also worth keeping in mind that it's typically the most judgemental people who happen to be leading unhappy lives. It is far easier for them to focus their attention on what other people are doing rather than spending time working on themselves.

FEAR OF PUBLIC SPEAKING

The Book of Lists by David Wallechinsky tells us that public speaking is the number one fear of adults—and ironically, death is number seven! So, when someone says they'd rather die than speak in public, they actually statistically mean it! The ability to communicate your thoughts and ideas effectively is essential in today's connected world. It's a skill that will benefit you greatly in both your personal and professional life. If strong communication is important for your career or an area you want to improve, two valuable resources provide a supportive and encouraging environment for skill development:

1. **Join a Toastmasters chapter** – an affordable option that helps you practice and refine your speaking skills.

2. **Take the Dale Carnegie course** – a more in-depth program that requires a greater financial investment in yourself.

Check with your employer, as they may offer financial assistance or even cover the cost entirely. Both options are widely available in most metropolitan areas, and depending on your location, you may find one closer than you expect.

Now, there's something I want to acknowledge: Because of technology like YouTube, TikTok, and other video platforms, many young adults today don't deal with this fear nearly as much as my generation (baby boomers) did. They grow up making and posting videos from a very young age, and many are very gifted communicators. If you don't believe me, look at the average age of most social media influencers or the TED Talk speakers! Of course, this is a very broad generalization and many of the people reading this book may still struggle in this area.

FEAR OF CHANGE

This particular topic may, in fact, be the central thesis of my next book. It is, without a doubt, a very real and very large part of WHY people at all ages stop growing. Ever heard this one? "I made up my mind to never read another book after college." Someone who maintains this kind of mindset is generally very uncomfortable with change. Interestingly enough, change and the speed at which it occurs is an everyday reality we all HAVE TO find a way to deal with in our lives as it now happens and continues to accelerate at "the speed of technology." I have heard that the amount of change our grandparents dealt with in their lifetime is the amount of change our current society deals with every year! This is called accelerating acceleration.

The best way to effectively deal with change is to first examine your attitude toward change. How do you see it? Then you must ask yourself why you feel that way. Once you have identified the answers to these questions, use the spaces below to unpack the issues and see what you can do to better deal with them. A mindset of total unwillingness to change will dramatically limit your growth potential, so if you're serious about developing your purpose, you really have to deal with it.

What's my attitude toward change?

_____

_____

Why do I feel this way?

_____

_____

What steps can I take to more effectively deal with change in my life?

_____

_____

If I do accept change, what's in it for me?

_____

_____

DOUBT VS BELIEF

Webster defines doubt as a feeling of uncertainty or lack of conviction. Personally, I believe it's one of the world's most often used tools to keep people from finding their purpose in life because it takes away the certainty of action. We can have all the good intentions in the world, but if we never act on them, nothing will happen. How do I know this? As previously mentioned, I've been planning to write this book for almost twenty years, but when it came down to it, I honestly couldn't see myself doing it. What changed? I started to believe I could write this book. Belief is the opposite of doubt just like faith is the opposite of fear. These two juxtapositions are the reason we will discuss the importance of what you allow into your mind and what you say to yourself.

Doubt causes indecision, hesitation, and procrastination. I'll do it tomorrow and yet tomorrow never comes. I've heard it said that "tomorrow is a day found only on the calendar of fools." While I know that's a rather harsh statement, I think most of us have been privy to instances where a doubter who tells everyone why it won't work or can't be done is often passed up by someone actually doing it. Overcoming doubt involves a combination of mindset shifts, practical strategies, and emotional resilience.

The most powerful component to overcoming doubt is to have vision. Embrace the idea that the possibilities are endless and visualize succeeding in your goals. Every amazing feat began with a vision, a dream of something big. As Napoleon Hill famously said in *Think and Grow Rich*, "Whatever the mind can conceive and believe, it can achieve."

> "YOU WILL NEVER ACCOMPLISH EVERYTHING YOU DREAM ABOUT. BUT, YOU WILL NEVER ACCOMPLISH ANYTHING YOU DON'T DREAM ABOUT FIRST."
> — Walt Disney

Question: How long has the physical property that governs flight been around? I think the actual "physics term" is called lift, which is what happens when the shape of the wing creates air flow, where the air over the top of the wing is moving faster than the air on the bottom, causing the plane to lift off the ground. So how long has the physical property of lift been around? Answer: Since creation, right? So if the physical property has been around forever, why did it take till December 17, 1903, for the Wright Brothers to perform the first successful powered flight? Because no one believed it could be done! "If man were meant to fly, God would have given him wings," is one of the more popular quotes of that time, anchored in the strong belief that man could not and should not fly.

These doubters lacked the vision of Orville and Wilbur Wright—or, if you want to go back a bit further, Leonardo da Vinci, whose drawings clearly identified his work on inventing the flying machine. Both believed and therefore developed the vision to create the flying machine. Think about how that one development changed the world and made it a much smaller place. Many historians consider the invention of powered flight one of the most important in history.

Does the name Roger Bannister ring a bell? He's credited as the first person to ever run a sub-four-minute mile. It happened on May 6, 1954, at the Iffley Road track in Oxford, England. His time was 3:59:4. In fact, by today's standards, that's a rather slow time as the current world record for the fastest mile is held by Hicham El Guerrouj of Morocco who, in 1999, set the record in Rome with a time of 3:43:13, a full 16:27 seconds faster than Bannister.

Before Banister broke the four-minute barrier for the mile, contemporary medical wisdom not only held that it was impossible for a person to do it, but that, according to studies published in medical journals of the time, a man's lungs lacked the capacity to properly oxygenate the body to accomplish this feat—so even if they actually did beat four minutes, they would die in the process. Everyone else believed that except Bannister. Even more interesting is that after Bannister did it, his record lasted only forty-six days! After he shattered the physical barrier, which I would argue is less important than the mental barrier, it's reported that as many as twenty-four other runners accomplished sub-four-minute miles very quickly after that.

Another component to overcoming doubt is preparation. Whenever I am well-prepared for something, whether it's a sporting event, a musical performance, or a presentation, I feel confident knowing I have taken the necessary steps to perform at my best. When I am underprepared, my confidence wanes, and not only does my performance suffer but my enjoyment of the task also diminishes.

Emotional resilience is paramount in kicking doubt to the curb. Understanding that you're going to make mistakes helps alleviate the pressure of any given task and allows more confidence to step forward. Begin seeing mistakes and setbacks as a necessary part of growth, and utilize them to course-correct and improve as you move forward.

Think about a time when you let doubt hold you back from pursuing something important to you. What were the specific doubts you had, and how did they affect your actions or decisions?

_____

_____

_____

_____

_____

_____

How do you currently handle mistakes or setbacks? Write about a time when a mistake helped you grow or led to a breakthrough. What can you do to shift your mindset and view setbacks as a valuable part of your growth?

_____

_____

_____

_____

How does preparation impact your confidence? Write about a time when you felt fully prepared for a task or challenge and how that preparation made a difference in your performance. How can you apply this to upcoming goals?

_____

_____

_____

_____

_____

What are some of your biggest dreams or goals? Take a moment to visualize your success. What does it feel like to achieve that goal? How can you use this vision to fuel your perseverance in the face of doubt?

_____

_____

_____

_____

_____

DEALING WITH AND OVERCOMING ADVERSITY

"IT'S OK TO FALL APART SOMETIMES. TACOS DO, AND
YET WE STILL LOVE THEM."
— Anonymous

If we are alive on planet Earth, we will have tough times and go through things that don't seem right or fair. It's not a question of if they will happen but when they will happen—the most important question is how we will deal with them. I have found that the valley moments are just as important as the mountaintop ones. When we are being tested in the valley, that's when our character is being forged. Effectively dealing with and overcoming adversity is a vital part of a life well lived on purpose.

Let me give you an example. My younger brother, Sean, went through a life-altering experience roughly a year ago, where in a period of three weeks, he completely lost his hearing! I've since learned it's called sudden hearing loss syndrome and is more common than you would expect. His doctor told him he sees roughly two people per month with this syndrome—and this in a town of less than one hundred thousand people. They believe the root cause is viral but don't know for sure, and he's been told it's very unlikely it will ever come back.

He will probably be getting a cochlear implant to restore his ability to hear, but before he does, he's trying a number of homeopathic remedies to see if he can regain any portion of his hearing. The primary reason for that is we've learned the implant provides a different type of hearing that you have to retrain your brain to get used to.

Personally, other than losing my sight, I can't think of anything more devastating to go through and am honestly blown away by how well he has handled the whole thing.

In his past work life, he has worked for the Tony Robbins organization and devoted plenty of his time to developing and maintaining a strong, positive attitude. He's always kept himself in good physical condition and has been a sensible eater.

Sean has had some really rough days trying to process and accept this new reality. His experience is a textbook example of someone who "always looks on the bright side of life," as the Art Garfunkel song goes. Up until this point, he has worked as a successful leader in the convenience store industry and hopes to return once he gets his hearing back. But the emotional, financial, and personal impact of this issue has tested him right to his very core. His experience highlights the powerful role that mindset, preparation, and adaptability play in overcoming adversity.

I can also attest to the pangs of adversity. Because of a bad back, I have often found myself lying in my adjustable bed (a necessity as you age), unable to walk or even support my body weight. I unknowingly injured my back at age seventeen carrying PA equipment, which at that time was very large and very heavy, out of my sister's wedding reception. That little click I heard in my back all those years ago has manifested itself into a lower back, L4 condition that requires weekly chiropractic care for me to be up on my feet and live a normal active life. Unfortunately, even with chiropractic care, I still experience intermittent catastrophic failures that always seem to occur at the worst possible time.

The root cause is a bulging disc, but almost anything can set it off. In a more recent experience, I was helping Tamela replant a few new flocks around the house's outside rock beds and out went my lower back, and down I went like a chopped down tree, howling in pain as I tumbled to the ground. If any of the neighbors were watching they got a really good show.

Lying on my back in the grass, I knew I had to cancel plans and contact my chiropractor to get a treatment plan in place. Unable to walk, I crawled across the lawn, through the rock beds, and up the stairs into bed. My wife ran a tub for me, and the buoyancy of water eased the pressure on my back.

These experiences have taught me the importance of preparing for anything life throws your way. Whether it's health, finances, or relationships, adversity will strike when you least expect it. The key is to stay calm, anticipate challenges, and develop a plan to move forward. We can't control what happens to us, but we can always control how we respond as the following diagram indicates.

OUT OF MY CONTROL

Changing people

People's perception of me

Other people's words

The past

Other people's actions

How I treat others

My actions

My words

Being present

How I respond

IN MY CONTROL

How other people feel

God's timing

My thoughts

Walking by faith

How I spend my time

Outcomes

My attitude

The opinions of others

How I take care of myself

Other people's choices

The weather

What tomorrow will bring

CONTROL DIAGRAM

So what can we learn from all this? First, as we'll discuss in the next chapter, attitude plays a huge part in dealing with adversity. Second, we have to focus only on what we can control and spend little or no time on things outside of our control, as illustrated above. Lastly, if you've never read Dale Carnegie's *How to Stop Worrying and Start Living*, please read it, especially if you are going through a difficult season in your life. It's a treasure trove of how to manage your mind while navigating adversity.

When faced with unexpected challenges, how do you typically react? Do you stay calm or do you let the situation control you?

_____

_____

_____

Reflect on a recent adversity you've faced. How did your attitude affect the outcome? How did you navigate that difficult moment?

_____

_____

_____

How can you apply the concept of focusing only on what you can control to your current circumstances? Are there areas where you are wasting energy on things outside your control?

_____

_____

_____

NOTES

_____

_____

_____

_____

_____

_____

_____

_____

_____

CHAPTER 5

THE IMPORTANCE OF ATTITUDE

In a very real sense, attitude is the lens or filter of your mind's eye that influences how you process and deal with life. I have a couple of interesting observations about life that I'd like to share. First, we only get one, so let's make the most of it! Second, life only moves one direction and that's forward. Last, the key is to view problem-solving as a gift, not a burden, and to welcome problems with a positive mental attitude. A person equipped with a positive mindset will accomplish great things.

Attitude is the elixir, the fairy dust, the magic formula, the difference maker—whatever descriptor you care to slap on it—that differentiates those who accomplish their purpose in life from those who don't.

In a sense, life is a series of problem-solving exercises. We will never be without problems in this life. Norman Vincent Peale, author of *The Power of Positive Thinking* and considered the father of the modern philosophy of positive mental attitude, was once visited by a very dejected young man who was dealing with a difficult problem.

Peale said, "Come with me, young man, and I'll show you a place where there are no problems!" The man eagerly followed Peale, who took him to the closest cemetery. "Well, here we are," Peale said. The young man asked with a puzzled look, "Why did you bring me to a cemetery?" Peale replied, "Because this is the only place you will ever find people who no longer have any problems, young man."

How can you change/improve your attitude? As mentioned earlier, your mind is like a computer, and what you put into it is what comes out. Therefore, we can change and improve our attitude by changing our input. Let's examine the sources of our input: what we read, what we listen to, what we watch, who we associate with, and how we see and talk to ourselves about ourselves. Determining the source of these inputs can prove very enlightening when we are self-reflecting.

WHY YOUR THOUGHTS MATTER

This simple flow chart identifies that the root of your character development starts with what you think about. For that reason, managing your thoughts and, equally if not more importantly, managing your input is the bedrock of changing and adjusting your attitude. Let's unpack this concept a little further and break it down into specific input categories that we can review.

What Do You Read?

This particular topic has changed my life more than any other. Through my involvement in entrepreneurial endeavors, I was introduced to a book titled *The Magic of Thinking Big* by David Schwartz. At twenty-three years of age, engaging with this book completely rocked my world! I had no idea there were different ways to think, positive or negative, small or big, hopeful or hopeless, optimistic or pessimistic, and that your mind is where all accomplishments begin.

Once I began to understand this, I had a number of key revelations. First, I realized I had a negative attitude. I honestly didn't know any different. Second, I began to quickly see the correlation between how people think and the direction their lives were moving. And lastly, I got really excited about my future because I realized that by managing my input, I could directly control and improve my output. Till then, I thought everything just sort of happened.

You will find a recommended reading list in the back of this book. It's up to you, of course, but if you are serious about truly identifying your purpose, select one of the titles, try reading it for fifteen minutes each evening before you fall asleep, and create a new habit. Do that for one year and I promise the new you won't even recognize the old you!

Please write down the name of the first book you will start reading and the date you start in the space below:

- _____Date: _____

What will be your next book?

- _____

WHAT DO YOU WATCH?

There is so much video input available to us in our smartphones these days. What are we allowing into one of the primary gateways of our minds? As parents, we understand the importance of not allowing our children to watch things that we know will be harmful to them, either immediately or in the future. However, so many adults completely undervalue using the same vigilance for themselves.

Personally, I avoid almost all new films and series on any of the streaming platforms as they routinely promote alternative lifestyles, promiscuity, adultery, extreme violence, very vulgar and profane language, and unbelievable plots that tend to focus on dark subjects—and because, in my opinion, they just plain stink.

Now, in full transparency, in my younger days, I had a mouth that could make a sailor blush. I loved all of the action films I could get my hands on—Chuck Norrris and Steven Seagal are still some of my favorites—so I'm not trying to say I'm a choir boy in this area. But what life has taught me is that it really does matter what you put in your mind. We all need to regularly examine this area and do our best to integrate more inputs from the uplifting, positive side than the really dark negative side.

Take an inventory of your daily screen time. Are you aware of how much time you spend on your phone each day? If you have a smartphone, you have built-in data of the total time you spend on screen each day. Find that data to record below (a simple Google search will help you find it in your settings).

Phone Screen Time: _____

Now add to that the average amount of time you spend watching TV.

Phone Screen Time: _____ + TV Screen Time _____

Write your total here: _____

For the next month, try swapping one hour of your total screen time with reading a growth mindset book, goal setting, or developing practices that will aid in living your purpose.

WHO'S IN YOUR CIRCLE?

Who do you associate with at work, both in person and virtually? As stated above, I have observed that many parents follow this principle very carefully for their children, "Don't hang around with them, they are a bad influence," yet completely ignore it in their own lives. We become like the people we associate with. It's part of the human condition. If you hang around criminals long enough, sooner or later you will become a criminal. If you are happily married, you may not want to spend all your time with people who are divorced.

> "WHOEVER WALKS WITH THE WISE BECOMES WISE,
> BUT THE COMPANION OF FOOLS WILL SUFFER HARM."
> — Proverbs 13:20

As an example of the power of association, have you ever played a sport with someone better than you and found yourself playing better overall? Or maybe you've watched professionals live and thought, *Oh, that's how that's done*, and were able to make an improvement in your own game?

Now, am I saying to stop spending time with all your friends or family or cut a bunch of people out of your life? Of course not! Just ask yourself this question: Are the people in my life lifting me up and helping me grow and develop or are they pulling me down and having a negative impact on my life, adding no value? Just be vigilant and mindful of who you are surrounding yourself with. All great leaders go to great lengths to surround themselves with the very best people they can find.

Finally, there's a story of a person driving down the road. They are crossing over a bridge and see someone just about to jump off. They pull their car over, sit and talk to the person for five minutes, and then both get up and jump off the bridge together. Be careful who you listen to and allow into your life.

Please don't misunderstand my message here. Of course, we want to be there and help others. Just don't let their problems become yours. With some people, we have to learn to "love them from a distance." The most vivid example I can think of is holiday family gatherings. Often, because of the many and varied personalities, we can only take them for a certain amount of time before it's time to go home. Many films have been made about this topic, so there must be some relevance here.

How can you be more intentional about surrounding yourself with people who uplift and encourage your development? Write down three specific actions you can take to cultivate this kind of association.

- _____

- _____

- _____

WHAT IS YOUR FOCUS?

What do you think about and allow your mind to focus on? The key word in this question is **allow**, as you have 100 percent control over your mind and what you think about. Now, I know some of you might protest, "No, I don't! You don't understand how my mind works and how I'm bombarded with all of these negative thoughts. My mind just seems to spin and spiral out of control." What you experience is not bad, many experience the same thing; I fully recognize that. We all deal with issues in this area. But I want to challenge you to think a bit more broadly. If you have allowed your mind to operate just as it wants to, you're reinforcing the patterns and it becomes part of your habit structure. However, with on-purpose thinking, you can change your thinking habit structure and thus you can change yourself.

The following poem was written by a young marine. He said, "There are two natures that beat within my chest, / One is foul, and one is blessed. / The one I love, and the other I hate, / But the one I FEED will DOMINATE." We all have these two little guys inside our heads constantly fighting with each other. Many people depict them as an angel on the right shoulder and a devil on the left.

Here's the question: Which one wins? Answer: The one who trains harder! If you feed your mind with dark, negative garbage, then by default you are training the devil inside of you. If you feed your mind with positive, uplifting, good things, then you are training the angel inside of you. Many experts have compared the human mind, the greatest, most complex creation on earth, by the way, to a computer— what you put into it you get back out. In other words, garbage in, garbage out.

Here's another great analogy: Your mind is like a video store filled with shelves of movies from your entire life—both the good and the bad. What plays most often on the screen of your mind? Positive moments or negative ones? When you try something new or push beyond your comfort zone, what do you pull up on that mental screen? Do you replay every time you've tried and failed, or do you focus on the moments when you pushed through fear and doubt and succeeded?

What thoughts or beliefs do you currently allow to dominate your mind, and how are they influencing your actions, emotions, and behaviors?

_____

_____

_____

How Do You See Yourself?

When you look in the mirror, what do you see? The honest answer to that question is vital because it will inform how we live a life on purpose. How we see ourselves touches our core beliefs on our ability to learn and grow. If we don't value ourselves, how can we expect anyone else to?

Did you know that 70 percent of the conversations you have on any given day take place inside? It's you talking to you. What are you saying to yourself? Are you lifting yourself up or tearing yourself down?

Here's a litmus test. Would you say to anyone else what you are saying to you about yourself? If the answer is "NO WAY, NEVER," then why are you saying it to yourself? Most people are highly critical of themselves and their self-talk is far more negative than what they'd ever say to anyone else. If this resonates with you, this is a major opportunity for improvement! If you wouldn't say to the person next to you *What were you thinking when you got dressed today? Man, you are so out of shape! Oh boy, another bad hair day today. That idea of yours will never work out! Why are you even trying to lose this weight? You never have before! Forget about that promotion, you've tried so many times before and they never select you! You're not smart enough. You're not good-looking enough…* and on and on. Why say such things to yourself? This is called negative self-talk.

Now, here is the great news about self-image: If it's not where we would like it to be, we have the power to change it by what we do moving forward. Remember, life is a journey that we live one day at a time, and we can control what we do each day to help ourselves move forward. In terms of our own personal growth, we are either moving forward in life or moving backward. There is no standing still. We either accept that reality and use it to our advantage or ignore it and allow life to run us.

> "HUMILITY DOESN'T MEAN THINKING LESS OF
> YOURSELF, IT MEANS THINKING OF YOURSELF LESS."
> — C.S. Lewis

Some of the most successful, on-purpose people I've ever met, read about, or heard speak all have one thing in common: They believed in themselves long before anyone else did, and a large part of that belief came from positive, uplifting self-talk. "Well, Mitch, you don't understand all I've been through, all the terrible things my own family has said about me, or well-meaning coach or guidance counselor or whoever." You're right, I don't. But I do know this: Like so many of us, you've allowed whatever those things were to get on the inside of you, you started believing them, and you spoke those things into existence in your life.

Think of it like this: You are walking down the road of life, and what your self-talk is saying to you and about you is literally paving the road in front of you. Is it being paved with garbage and negative "can't do" thoughts that are leaving potholes everywhere? Or is it being paved with "can do" thoughts and words of praise, affirmations: "I am well able," "I expect tomorrow to be better than today," "I can do all things through Him who strengthens me," "I will lend and not borrow," "I see myself as God sees me," "I am a child of The King!" These words create a smooth road on which to walk all the days of your life. Believe it or not, this particular issue is 100 percent under your control. No one else but you gets to tell you what to say to you. Keep and store up the good and evict the bad!

If you've never done it before, slow down and listen to what you are saying to yourself inside and out for one day. Then write down what you heard below:
What do you say when you first wake up?

_____

What do you tell yourself in preparation for your work day?

_____

What do you say to yourself before you begin an important meeting or presentation?

_____

What do you say to yourself after a day's work?

_____

What thoughts do you have about tomorrow as you drift off to sleep?

_____

If you don't like any of the answers you wrote down, making adjustments and changes in this one area of your life will do more than you can possibly imagine. You are the one who has to make them, though, because only you know what your self-talk sounds like. Trust me on this one. If you flip the switch from can't to can, negative to positive, put your seatbelt on and "Katie, bar the door,"—look out world, here YOU come!

EMBRACE YOUR OWN KINDA CRAZY

As human beings on planet Earth, we all have our own unique looks, voices, and behavior patterns that I like to call "our own kinda crazy." These play an important part in how we see ourselves and how we interact with and perceive others. In my case, anxiety disorders run deep through my family line, and both my parents and my siblings have had to learn to navigate life while dealing with this particular set of issues.

It hit me hardest in my late twenties after my dad had suffered his first heart attack. For some reason, that event was a trigger for my anxiety disorder. After struggling with it for many years, I finally found medications that could help me control and manage it.

What I have learned from "my own kinda crazy" is that it has enhanced and refined many of my gifts and strengths. I sincerely believe that my intense need for repetition and my deep desire to master something when I set out to learn it have shaped many areas of my life where I excel today.

In today's terms, that's called being passionate about something. Earlier in my life, I was often labeled a fanatic about anything that truly interested me. Whatever you want to call it, I'm confident that when you reflect and embrace "your own kinda crazy," it will serve you well—just as it has for me.

Reflect on "your own kinda crazy." What unique quirks, habits, or tendencies make you who you are? Consider how these aspects of yourself could shape your strengths or guide your passions and ultimately help you discover your purpose.

_____

_____

_____

_____

CULTIVATE AN ATTITUDE OF GRATITUDE

You don't have to look very far to find someone else who wishes they had your life! I recall a quote by author Dennis Waitley: "I had the blues because I had no shoes until upon the street, I met a man who had no feet." A large part of gratitude is realizing how blessed we really are. Regardless of what you may hear from a growing number in our current national conversation, the good old USA is still the greatest country in the world, and we won the birth lottery being born here.

I offer two pieces of evidence. One, if this country were such a terribly oppressive and rotten place to live, why have so many people risked life and limb to come here? Second, all you have to do is travel abroad to any third-world country and you will very quickly see with your own eyes how good our standard of living is on every level compared with theirs.

My first experience traveling to a third-world country took place in my late twenties, when my wife and I visited Tijuana, Mexico, just across our southern border, with my sister and brother-in-law when they lived in San Diego, California. The main streets where businesses and restaurants existed for the tourists were in reasonable shape. But all you had to do was peer down a few side streets where you would see nothing but shacks and poverty. Once again, Michael, my brother-in-law, our guide, ensured we understood that it was unsafe to venture down these alleys lest we end up a "missing person" with our face on a milk cartoon.

We had a similar experience in other vacation spots in Mexico where we had to run the gauntlet of getting through the airport from the plane to our curbside transportation. The neighborhoods we passed through on the way to these resort oases were very run down. Once on property, after going through a security checkpoint, they don't come right out and say it, but you are strongly encouraged to remain on the property at all times during your stay.

In addition, a number of family members have gone on mission trips to Belize and literally kissed the ground when they got back to the USA. Lastly, our church supports a mission church in Costa Maya. Many of my church friends who have visited Costa Maya to help build the mission church and assist in other ways often return deeply moved, marveling at how those with so little can radiate such joy, and reflecting on how truly fortunate we are to live in the United States.

So, with all that in mind, let's count our blessings. What are you grateful for?

- _____

- _____

- _____

- _____

- _____

- _____

If you struggled to come up with five things, let this be a sign to begin practicing gratitude every day. There are so many things we take for granted. And regardless of your current circumstances, there are always things for which to be grateful. It's a way of looking at the world.

Here is the list of things that I am grateful for in my life:

- My relationship with Jesus.
- My wife. I know God selected her for me and she is my greatest blessing on this earth and the most important relationship I have.
- My children and their health.
- My and my wife's health.

- My grandchildren! Being a grandparent is the best club to be a member of on the planet!
- My gifts from God.
- The fact that I live in the United States of America.
- My career. I am blessed to work in an industry that has provided my family with a very good living. I am also blessed to work for a financially solid company that is made up of great people.
- My new team leader. She is a wonderful person and a real joy to work with.
- This book, as I believe it's through the hand of God and can make a difference for His Kingdom.

Are people happier to see you coming or going? An interesting question, don't you think? The answer to this question is a very important one, and if it's the latter, you may have another opportunity for improvement and want to examine your attitude. I suspect even asking this question brings certain people to mind as we all know people on both ends of this spectrum. But let's be really candid and transparent here, very few people want to be around people who have a poor attitude, except, perhaps other people with poor attitudes, then they don't have to have someone regularly telling them it's all going to work out.

Attitude equals altitude, which means that people with good attitudes generally tend to rise higher in their lives and have a much higher chance of fully determining and accomplishing their purpose in life. Why? Well, most likely because they believe it can be done. That's what helps them get started, stay focused, disciplined, and on mission to fully accomplish their purpose. And equally important, if not more so, they view problems, challenges, and issues through a positive lens.

"THE PESSIMIST SEES THE DIFFICULTY IN
EVERY OPPORTUNITY; THE OPTIMIST SEES THE
OPPORTUNITY IN EVERY DIFFICULTY."
-Sir Winston Churchill

Notes

_____

_____

_____

_____

_____

_____

_____

_____

_____

_____

PURPOSE THROUGH VISION AND CREATIVITY

Purpose is the driving force behind vision and creativity. When we uncover our true purpose, it often unlocks a wellspring of creative energy we didn't know existed. I've experienced this time and again in my life—as a sales professional, a communicator, or, more recently, an author. It's also been central to my journey as a musician. And while the term "professional musician" might sound impressive, let me clarify—it simply means I was paid to play, though not paid very well, as a coffeehouse and lounge performer back in the day. Nonetheless, the connection between purpose and creativity has been a constant in shaping my path.

PURPOSE THROUGH ARTISTRY

I always start with the title of anything I am working to create. For some reason, once I develop a clear title, everything else follows. It's the way I've written all my songs, including "Together You and I," "Carpenter's Son," "Through the Eyes of A Child," and "Growing in the Grace of God." It's also the way I framed up the content for this book and will do for future books as well.

When my oldest daughter, Taylor, was in first grade at Mt. Hope Lutheran School, her teacher asked me to write a song because she had seen me sing and play regularly at our church (the school and church shared the same building). She shared the theme for the children's upcoming program, "growing in the grace of God." Any guess as to what I named the song I wrote for them? You got it! "Growing in the Grace of God." Once I had the title in my mind, all I needed to do was add a simple melody that was very much like a round (Row, Row Your Boat) and the words and chords. It was ready to go over the weekend.

If memory serves, I recorded the finished song on a CD and sent it in with Taylor. The kids used that to learn and practice the song. When it came time to present it together, we connected before the service to practice it for the very first time. Other than a minor (but loud) pre-performance issue, it came off very well and was well received by all. All glory to God on that as He's where it came from in the first place.

I remember feeling particularly proud of that moment as it was the first and only time I ever composed something and performed it with a group of people on the guitar as the accompanist, not the lead vocalist.

As another example of purpose and artistry, I was sitting in a mobile home in 1983 that I rented with a roommate who had two big German Shepherds he often forgot to let out, if you catch my drift. I was in Bemidji, Minnesota, working for Kmart.

I had promised my then-fiancé Tamela that I'd write an original song for our wedding. I had my usual macaroni and cheese with sliced hot dogs on a paper plate in front of me (the single man's delight) and was looking to deepen my faith walk at that time. So I prayed, "Lord, I promised Tamela I'd write a song for our wedding and I really need your help." Into my mind popped the following lyric: "As we stand before the altar both together hands entwined, as we look to new horizons looking out beyond this time…" I thought, hmm… this is really good! I grabbed my legal pad, red-tipped felt pen and the lyrics just flowed out. The entire song was written and finished in forty-five minutes, including the guitar part. I can attest, especially at that time in my life, that I was not what you'd characterize as a poet. This experience was where I had my very first inkling that there may be a connection between purpose and creativity; when my purpose has been on point (in this case, I was about to marry my best friend and fiancé), my creativity comes with ease.

In 1995, Tamela and I wrote a song together titled "Through the Eyes of a Child" for our first daughter's baptism. I had a really good start on the lyrics and asked for Tamela's input on finishing the verse and refrain on a road trip home to visit her family. We started talking through different ideas on what we wanted the song to say and how important it was that the miracle of adoption be the red thread that ran through the lyrics. By the time we got to her parent's house, the lyrics were complete and the melody came soon after, as Taylor's baptism was quickly approaching. It's been one of my most requested songs over the years and I have been asked to perform it at a number of other family members' baptisms.

Working hard for something we don't care about causes us stress. On the flip side, working hard for something we love ignites our passion! Use passion as part of your tool kit to discover your true purpose. I've also heard that if you love what you do, you'll never work a day in your life. Another way of saying that in the context of this book is, if you stay on purpose with your life's work, you will never work a day in your life.

Prompt: Purpose Through Artistry

Do you carve out time to sit quietly with your thoughts? If so, do you journal? If not, make a plan to create quiet space during the day.

_____

_____

_____

_____

In what ways do you allow your creative self to play? If you aren't currently setting aside creative time, make a plan to do so.

_____

_____

_____

_____

Purpose Through Vision

"IF YOU DON'T SEE YOURSELF DOING IT,
YOU NEVER WILL."

— Xander Schauffele, 2024 PGA & Open Champion

As a passionate but average tennis player in my youth, I think back to some of the best matches I played and some of the best shots I made. In almost every case, I can remember seeing the shot in my mind's eye just a moment before I struck the ball—and the ball went and did exactly what I saw before I hit it. Sports psychologists have called this phenomenon many things over the years, but in my day, we called it being in the zone!

I have had the same kind of experience on the golf course as well, again only being an average golfer at best. I saw the line on the putt and the ball rolling into the hole a split second before I hit it—and voila! I sunk the putt. The same thing has happened on an important drive, approach shot or chip. Most recently, I was playing at Stonebrooke here in the south Metro area with three other players. We started on ten that day and I was playing OK on the first few holes, but then I drained a longer putt for a birdie on a par five.

And guess what? I had the same exact experience as I described above. I saw it happen in my head first, then on the front nine, I went on a tear where I birdied two of the par threes back to back, the last one with a chip in from off the green. As I stood over the chip, I pictured what I wanted the shot to look like and that's exactly how it came off my club. A beautiful arching shot with just the right amount of pace. It trundled down to the hole, took the break at the last second, and dove right into the cup! The other guys started going crazy—and of course so did I! I hadn't chipped in off the green like that in decades.

Vision is the ability to see something in your mind before it happens, and it plays an important role in everyone's life. It is a large part of what helps us bring our purpose from concept or plan into physical reality.

PROMPT: PURPOSE THROUGH VISION

What are your dreams for the future?

_____

_____

_____

_____

What does a typical day look like in your ideal life?

_____

_____

_____

_____

What about your current lifestyle will prevent you from reaching these goals?

_____

_____

_____

_____

LINDSAY'S STORY

The below is written by my editor and publisher, Lindsay Bednar, about her transformative journey of finding her purpose.

I knew from a young age that I was here to make an impact. In my younger years, I fantasized that I would be a famous singer or musician. In high school, I was certain I would become a part of the cast of Saturday Night Live. On the surface, you'd maybe think I wanted fame. However, I had a deeper knowing that I was made to make connections with people in a creative way—but I didn't know that it would take me years to figure out.

In my senior year of high school, I became overwhelmed with the idea that I had to choose my path in life in order to figure out what I was going to do next—so much so that I developed shingles (a condition I later learned is often brought on by stress). My mom suggested I go into education; after all, my grandmother and her two sisters were teachers and it was a dependable career that would allow me summers off with my future children. I figured that was a solid choice and enrolled at St. Cloud State to attend their education program.

Once I graduated, I got cold feet about teaching. I spent most of my senior year of college grading and editing papers, and the onslaught of work while my friends were out on Friday and Saturday nights was too much. I worked as an administrative assistant for about a year until that proved to be understimulating, and I found myself substitute teaching until I could land a permanent teaching position.

The substitute positions that were typically open were at alternative schools. These are the schools for students who fall behind in credits at the high school. While there are a myriad of reasons a student can fall behind, I quickly found that many of these students came from tough backgrounds. Initially, they tried to push me away and saw me as another authority figure to be resisted. Honestly, I was terrified. I came from a small town in northern Minnesota and hadn't been exposed to much. I couldn't wrap my head around the behavioral issues and lack of respect. But little by little, I got to know the students.

One of my favorite units was when I had my students write their memoirs. I was blown away by the resilience these students showed every day. Some of them took care of their siblings in the evenings. Some worked after school until almost midnight to help support their family. Some dealt with parents who battled addiction and a home life that was pure chaos. Others had experienced unimaginable things at their young ages and yet continued to show up to school each day. I began to understand why they operated the way they did, and I learned firsthand the incredible resilience of humanity.

I never felt like teaching was going to be my thing. I never liked the structure of it—I didn't know it at the time but I had an entrepreneurial spirit, I just knew it felt too designated to me. But what kept me coming back were the stories of these kids and the ability to be a positive mentor to encourage them to keep going no matter what life was throwing their way. I loved when students came back years after graduating to tell me how they had carved a better life for themselves than the one they grew up in. But it wasn't until I had an idea for a book that I started to see my life going in another direction.

I was opening my emails during a prep hour and received a notification for a contest where, if you could articulate what home means to you, you could win $2,500. I decided to give it a whirl. As I began to write, the words flowed through me, almost as if they were coming from someplace, or someone, else. Although the book idea was a simplistic rhyme scheme for a children's book, I could feel deep in my soul when I finished writing that these words were going to be a book and it was going to change the trajectory of my life.

I drove home in complete silence that day. I was filled with ideas for follow-up books, I felt inspired, and, although I had no idea how I was going to turn my words into a book, I was determined to figure it out. Over the next several months, I absorbed everything I could about publishing, and ultimately, I decided I was going to create my own imprint to put out my own books. I took the names of my two greatest writing influences—my grandfather, Rodney, and my mom, Luann Kay—and named my publishing company Rodney K Press.

Initially, I had no intention of carrying other people's books, but after my first book came out, I had people reaching out asking if they could hire me to help bring theirs to life. Suddenly, things started to come together. I could take my love of and knack for writing and storytelling and combine it with my experience in teaching to guide others in the incredible journey I just had. My purpose was becoming clearer.

While I continued teaching for several more years, I was also growing my publishing company and bringing more books to life. It wasn't until 2020 when the world shut down and we all had more time to think about how we wanted our lives to look from day to day that I truly reassessed my career. While I loved working with the teens in the school, my own kids were getting older and busier and I wanted as much flexibility in my schedule as possible. I was also missing a creative outlet that teaching did not provide me. So, after that spring semester, I hung up my teaching hat and stepped into publishing full-time.

I've learned that my purpose lies heavily in connection and helping people tell their stories. As I have deepened into that purpose, I have also created a podcast called Storytelling. I lose track of time when I am meeting with a client or listening to a podcast guest share their story. That is a tell-tale sign of living in your purpose. In addition to that, I've found that opportunities come to me with ease the more I do things that are in alignment with my purpose. This is how we are all created to be! When we are utilizing our passion and offering our unique gifts to the world, everything flows with ease. That is our birthright. And I hope you find that, too.

OFTEN, THE PERSON YOU HELP THE MOST BY HELPING SOMEONE ELSE IS YOU!

— Mitch Larson

NOTES

IT'S NEVER TOO LATE

This chapter addresses a very real concern many people have, which is: How can I find and develop purpose at my age? This chapter holds a very special interest for me because of something I've observed in people of retirement age—my grandparents on both sides, my parents' sphere of influence, my parents themselves, and many aunts and uncles. Here it is: Those who retired with a purpose almost always outlived those who retired without one, and they enjoyed a happier, more fulfilling retirement.

Whether it was specific plans to travel, a plan to help their children accomplish something or assist with child care, launching their own business, spending quality time improving on a hobby (golf is a sport for a lifetime and a favorite of many) or volunteering their time to help someone else, when people in retirement have a fulfilling reason to get up every morning, their lives are happier, healthier and longer.

The purpose of this chapter is to illustrate that it's never too late to find your purpose. If you're not dead, you're not done. Let's look at a few people's lives at various ages and stages and draw wisdom and hope from their experiences of living on purpose. I've said it before, but I'll say it again: If you love what you do, you'll never work a day in your life. I submit that they simply identified their purpose and that created the LOVE for what they were doing. It's a bit like how you feel when you listen to one of your favorite songs, watch a movie, or return to a favorite place.

PURPOSE IN YOUR YOUTH

On a recent Billy Joel SiriusXM broadcast, they played all the songs from his albums in alphabetical order… a rather amazing feat, by the way, as you need a very substantial catalog to have your own station with enough music to play for any duration.

When asked about the song "James" off his 1976 Turnstiles album, he said; "This is a song about some people I knew, none of them actually named James, not following their path in life and opting for a more traditional path of education and employment and basically observing how miserable they were." He said, "I knew at 14 years old what I wanted to do and that I was going to be a professional musician and NOTHING was going to stop me from that!" Talk about the power of purpose in your youth! Billy Joel is unquestionably one of the most successful and purposeful musicians of modern notoriety. He recently completed a ten-year residency at Madison Square Garden, where virtually every show was sold out despite very expensive ticket prices. Billy Joel remains one of the most beloved and popular musicians of our time who clearly identified his purpose in his youth.

Perhaps one of the best examples of finding purpose in your youth is Eldrick Tont "Tiger" Woods, born December 30, 1975, and arguably one of the best-known athletes on the planet. The list of his accomplishments in golf is too long to mention, but there are two that encompass the breadth and depth of his golfing career: He is tied for the most wins on the PGA tour with Sam Snead at eighty-two and is second only to Jack Nicklaus in men's major championships with fifteen titles; Nicklaus has eighteen and remains the leader in major titles.

Tiger's life, from early childhood to the present, is one of the greatest examples of discovering purpose early on and building a clear mission and vision to achieve it. By setting measurable goals and breaking them into daily, manageable actions, he developed a habit structure that has become a model for many of today's aspiring athletes.

As an example of Tiger's focus, drive, and purpose, I recently heard a YouTube video of a clinic he was giving during a pro-am event. He said that in preparation for any tournament he's playing, he aims to have one thousand touches of the club per day to maintain his feel for the ball/club relationship. That doesn't mean one thousand balls hit per day, but a combination of woods, irons, chipping, pitching, and putting. Despite already being one of the greatest golfers of all time, he continues to put in relentless practice because he understands the power of habit and hard work.

Without a doubt, Tiger's most significant accomplishment was his fifteenth major championship victory, where he earned his fifth green jacket at The Masters in April 2019. This win was particularly remarkable because it ended an eleven-year drought since his last major victory at the 2008 US Open. In my opinion, that 2008 win ranks as his second greatest achievement, as he secured the title in a dramatic 18-hole play-off against Rocco Mediate—while playing on a broken leg.

Woods began his 2019 Masters win by entering Sunday's weather-shortened broadcast two shots back of the leader, Francesco Molinari, the pride of the Italian golfing world, and they went off as threesomes in the morning, aiming to finish before a major weather event hit. While Tiger didn't take off on a tear and win by double digits as had been his signature move in earlier days, what he did do was stay steady and close to the top of the leader board until hole twelve, the world-renowned par 3 at Augusta, "the prettiest little graveyard in sports." Two of the players in the group ahead "rinsed their balls" in Ray's Creek, resulting in double bogeys or higher, and both Molinari and Tony Finau hit their balls in the water while Tiger, because of his Masters' experience, played to the center of the green directly over the bunker on twelve via Jack Nicklaus' advice and made a difficult two-putt for par.

He walked on to the twelfth green two shots back and walked off the twelfth green with a one-shot lead. Now, if you take into account the fact that he had his back fused six months earlier, he wasn't sure he would ever even walk again, much less compete in golf at the highest level, and you have the greatest comeback of all time in major championship golf history. The magnitude of his achievement earned him the Presidential Medal of Freedom later that year, with many historians hailing it as one of the greatest accomplishments in all of sports.

Without his overarching purpose in life to become the greatest golfer of all time, he never would have persevered through all the pain, recovery, necessary work, and practice to get back to the point where he could achieve this unprecedented accomplishment.

PROMPT: PURPOSE IN YOUR YOUTH

Think back to when you were a kid, old enough to have dreams of the future. What did you want to be? What stopped you from pursuing that career or lifestyle?

_____

_____

_____

_____

_____

PURPOSE IN EDUCATION

Finding purpose in higher education often begins with curiosity and a willingness to explore. For example, a student who enters college unsure of their direction might take an introductory psychology course and become fascinated by human behavior. This curiosity could lead them to volunteer at a mental health center, where they realize their passion for helping others. Over time, they might decide to pursue a career in counseling or social work, discovering a deep sense of purpose in guiding others toward healing and self-discovery.

Another student might find purpose through extracurricular activities. A business major who joins a student-run entrepreneurship club may discover a love for leadership and innovation. By working on real-world projects, networking with professionals, and even launching a small startup, they gain hands-on experience that solidifies their desire to build businesses that create jobs and improve communities. Without actively engaging in these opportunities, they might have never realized how fulfilling entrepreneurship could be.

Sometimes, purpose is found in unexpected places. A student studying literature might take a creative writing class as an elective and discover a talent for storytelling. Encouraged by a professor, they begin writing poetry or short stories, eventually realizing that their true calling is to inspire others through words. This realization might lead them to change majors, pursue a writing career, or use their storytelling skills in another field such as marketing, journalism, or publishing.

Ultimately, higher education provides a unique space for students to explore, challenge themselves, and connect with experiences that shape their future. By staying open to new opportunities, embracing challenges, and seeking guidance from mentors, students can uncover a sense of purpose that aligns with their passions and strengths.

Are you satisfied with your educational path? If so, how has it helped you in pursuit of your purpose?

_____

_____

_____

_____

If not, is there schooling or training you desire to take that would further lead you to your pursuit of fulfilling your purpose?

_____

_____

_____

_____

PURPOSE WITHIN A CAREER

Many people define themselves, especially men, by their career: "Hi, I'm a lawyer (or teacher/engineer/etc)," or "I'm in sales, own a dry cleaning business, or a construction company," or "I'm in the office furniture business," etc. Far too many people see their job as simply that: a job—but conversely, if you are passionate about your work, it won't feel like work at all.

As mentioned in the introduction, I have talked to many people and heard a number of speakers and pastors talk about reaching the pinnacle in their particular field only to find it completely unfulfilling. When we approach our work simply as a source of income, as the story about my Kmart store manager in Chapter 1 did, we will undoubtedly feel drained by our work responsibilities, often resentful, and lack fulfillment in the day-to-day grind.

So, if approximately one-third of our life is spent working, how happy can we be if we are miserable one-third of our life? Not very happy, is the readily available answer, and I'd bet we all know people who fit this description. If that happens to be you, how can we help you find more purpose in what you do?

We've all met people who pour their hearts and souls into their careers because it truly is their purpose, like my wife's hair stylist Lori. They may have remained single, are widowed, and/or don't have children. Their work is their service to humanity and they make the world a better place because of how they add value in their careers. Think of the nurses, teachers, firefighters, or the food shelf managers of the world. Every single day they are making a positive impact with the service they provide through their careers.

I mentioned in Chapter 4 that I see a chiropractor regularly to hold my back together and keep me upright and in one piece. I have been doing so since the late 1980s when Dr. Gary Pennebaker was my regular chiropractor—another hometown hero I had the privilege of knowing.

Gary was a quiet man who let the way he lived his life and how he used his time speak for him. He was an honored Eden Prairie Lions Club member, serving as chapter president a number of times during his tenure. He also believed that chiropractic was his true purpose in life. Healing and keeping people in their best possible health was his way of serving the Lord.

We lost Gary in his late sixties because of an enlarged heart, and the sheer number of people at his celebration of life, with story after story about the way he quietly touched and impacted their lives, was a testimony to Gary's well-lived life on purpose.

What can we learn from the above stories? First, some people can identify their purpose early in life and spend a lifetime fulfilling it, as in the case of Tiger Woods. Second, for others, it takes more time and life experience to discover their purpose—perhaps during high school—setting them on a specific path, such as pursuing higher education to become a doctor or studying occupational therapy, as our youngest daughter Anya did.

Sometimes people don't truly identify their purpose until they are already in their chosen profession. When our girls were still school-age, we enrolled them in the Lutheran Church closest to the new home we had just moved into. We really loved the welcoming spirit of the congregation and got to be friends with the new pastor.

Turns out, this was his first assignment out of seminary as a new pastor. I noticed he was a bit more middle-aged and when I asked him about this being his first time pastoring, he told me he left the medical field where he was previously a doctor of anesthesiology, one of the more highly paid medical professions I've been told.

When I asked him what led him into ministry, he simply said, "I knew in my heart that being a pastor is what I'm supposed to be doing."

I then asked, "Did you consider ministry before medical school?"

He replied, "No, I didn't. I went into medicine to help people, and after several years as an anesthesiologist, I realized I had gotten way off track. I wasn't helping people in the way I truly wanted to, so a new vision was born in me—and here I am. My old friends and many family members think I'm crazy for walking away from such a well-paying and prestigious career, but I couldn't be happier. This is what I was born to do!"

PROMPT: PURPOSE WITHIN A CAREER

Here are a few questions that all of us should ask ourselves when we want to add more value to others in our chosen professions. And remember, the person you always help the most when you help others is you:

Is there a different audience you can redirect some of your time and effort to that will make a difference for them? For example, perhaps you are a golf pro and could help with your local First Tee programs?

_____

_____

_____

Is there an additional skill you could work to acquire within your field that would bring you more fulfillment and help others in the process?

_____

_____

_____

Is there a different department, division, or area in your career that would challenge you and reignite a passion and purpose that you've been unwilling to pursue because of any of the obstacles we discussed in Chapter 4?

_____

_____

_____

If you belong to a team, what can you do each day to ensure that your team members feel supported, seen, and appreciated?

_____

_____

_____

If you hold a management or leadership position, what are you doing to encourage your colleagues to grow and evolve?

_____

_____

_____

If you are an entrepreneur, how are you serving your client or customer base to ensure they are taken care of?

_____

_____

_____

What part of you is uniquely gifted in providing a positive climate each day?

_____

_____

_____

PURPOSE WITHIN THE HOME

I think most of us clearly see our families as the foundation for all of our accomplishments in life; I know I certainly do. It's what gets me up every morning and out the door to do whatever it takes to provide the best possible standard of living I can for them. Family is both a responsibility and a privilege—a source of strength that inspires us to push through challenges, persevere in tough times, and celebrate milestones, big or small. Through my example, I strive to equip my children with the tools they need for success in their lives, whether it's teaching them the value of hard work, the importance of integrity, or the necessity of resilience in the face of obstacles.

When we have a family to care for, our purpose takes on greater clarity and weight. It's no longer just about personal fulfillment; it's about being a role model, a provider, and a source of emotional and spiritual support. If you are blessed with a family of your own, purpose is a lot easier to come by because you have a tangible, deeply rooted reason to grow, learn, and strive for excellence. Family grounds us while simultaneously lifting us up, encouraging us to become the best version of ourselves—not just for our sake but for theirs. It's in the moments of shared laughter, quiet support, and collective effort that we find the truest and most enduring meaning in our lives.

PROMPT: PURPOSE WITHIN THE HOME
What role does family play in your sense of purpose?

_____

_____

_____

_____

PURPOSE IN YOUR SPIRITUAL LIFE

Finding purpose in your spiritual life is one of the most profound and fulfilling journeys you can undertake. It offers a sense of connection to something greater than yourself, grounding you in a world that often feels chaotic and unpredictable. Spirituality helps you explore life's deeper questions—why you are here, what truly matters, and how you can live in alignment with your values. Through prayer, meditation, or other practices, you cultivate a relationship with the divine or the universe, finding guidance and strength that transcends the limitations of the physical world.

Spiritual purpose often manifests as a calling to serve others, to live with compassion, and to pursue inner peace. It reminds you that your life is part of a larger tapestry, where even small actions can have lasting significance. In this way, spiritual purpose not only nourishes your soul but also informs how you interact with others and how you contribute to the world.

PROMPT: PURPOSE IN YOUR SPIRITUAL LIFE

Reflect on how your relationship with your spirituality shapes your sense of purpose. Are there practices or beliefs that have guided your decisions and actions so far? How can you deepen your connection to your spiritual path? Also, see the Invitation portion in the back of the book to delve deeper into a conversation about spirituality.

_____

_____

_____

_____

MAINTAINING YOUR PURPOSE

It's comforting to know that regardless of the way our lives go, we can always find purpose. Many of us start our lives going down one road but because of a variety of circumstances, that road ends and we are forced to find meaning in alternate ways. I have encountered several people who reiterate this point, their stories proving that we are capable of redefining our purpose no matter what life throws our way.

I first met Billy McKinney while assisting at a management training seminar during my tenure with Dale Carnegie. We connected immediately, exchanged contact information, and stayed in touch. Billy even joined our direct-selling business for a short time as an independent business owner because the concept of buying from yourself instead of the store really resonated with him.

We shared an interest in tennis and played together once—a match that left a lasting impression on me. Billy's athleticism was a window into his remarkable discipline and intensity. At six feet tall, his NBA career wasn't built on height but on relentless energy, earning him the nickname "The Crazed Hummingbird." Throughout our game on the tennis court, he ran down every shot, even leaping onto the grandstand bench to return what I thought was a winning backhand. I don't think I even hit his return shot. I just stood there with an astonished look on my face asking myself how on earth did he just do that.

After he won the match (a fairly even match, I might add), Billy explained the mindset required to succeed in professional sports. "It's a bit like a switch that gets flipped when the game starts," he said, highlighting the discipline, commitment, and intensity that set elite players apart from the rest.

But Billy's drive didn't end with his NBA career, which spanned seven years on teams like the Kansas City Kings, Utah Jazz, Denver Nuggets, San Diego Clippers, and Chicago Bulls. His alma mater, Northwestern University, retired his number in March 2024. He was not only a successful ball player but transitioned into operations and scouting positions for several teams, including the Minnesota Timberwolves, and was responsible for adding many key players to team rosters, including Scottie Pippen and Horace Grant for the Chicago Bulls and Giannis Antetokounmpo for the Milwaukee Bucks.

What's remarkable about Billy is how he continually found new ways to channel his purpose. In 2019, he was elected as mayor of his beloved hometown of Zion, Illinois. Billy's executive and leadership skills, willingness to always give 110 percent, and positive attitude help propel him to success in every endeavor he's pursued. His life is a testament to the power of purpose—an apt illustration showing that those who focus on finding their purpose will continue to lead fulfilling lives, no matter the age or occupation.

Another one of my and Tamela's hometown heroes is Tamela's sister Cindy. She embodies the term servant leader, always going above and beyond for others and constantly seeking opportunities to connect with and serve people. If you were to put Cindy in a crowd of strangers, most—if not all—would be her friend by the end of the day. Not only that, she remembers their names, their children's names, and the next time she sees them, she calls them by name, and asks about their kids.

I've known Cindy as long as I have known my wife, and she's always been this way—making lifelong friends wherever she goes. We were privileged to be the maid of honor and best man at her and her husband, Jim's, wedding, and we have shared many business and family vacation trips.

Tragically, Cindy lost Jim to esophageal cancer after thirty-seven years of marriage. Throughout the whole experience, both she and Jim carried themselves with incredible grace and peace, demonstrating unwavering faith in God's plan. Cindy has found strength in knowing that Jim is now home with our Lord and Savior, and she has used that truth as the cornerstone of her faith walk both during and after his passing.

Despite losing the love of her life, Cindy has continued to live with purpose. She served as a board member and now adviser for the Southwest MN chapter of Young Life, a Christ-centered ministry that builds relationships with young adults in their schools, at games, and in their everyday lives, ultimately with the aim of introducing them to Jesus. She first became involved when her son Luke was introduced to the program in high school, and her dedication has remained unwavering. Cindy is also deeply involved with her church and family, and she often says she knows this is exactly what God wants her to be doing. She exemplifies a life built on purpose.

It's never too late to fulfill your purpose. Human beings are made to accomplish things; it's how we are wired. What it is you are made to accomplish is uniquely yours and is why you are reading this book. The overarching message of this chapter is simply to point out that gaining experiences in life leads to a wider, better-rounded perspective, and it's not uncommon at all for anyone to truly identify their purpose a little later down life's path.

What will you do differently as a result of reflecting on this chapter?

_____

_____

_____

"IT'S NEVER TOO LATE TO BECOME WHO YOU WANT
TO BE. I HOPE YOU LIVE A LIFE THAT YOU'RE PROUD
OF, AND IF YOU FIND THAT YOU'RE NOT, I HOPE YOU
HAVE THE STRENGTH TO START OVER."
— F. Scott Fitzgerald

Notes

_____

_____

_____

_____

_____

_____

_____

_____

_____

_____

CHAPTER 8

A LIFE WELL-LIVED

The greatest gift any of us can leave our children and families is the gift of a solid legacy. In this chapter, I want to share insights on how purpose contributes to a life well-lived and finishing well, sowing a legacy of purpose in our lives for the coming generations to grow and build on. The dictionary defines legacy as the lasting influence of a person or thing. This kind of legacy isn't about material possessions or accomplishments; though they generally go hand in hand, it's about the values, principles, and purpose- driven actions that have shaped—the lives of those we love. By living with intention and aligning our lives with meaningful purpose, we create a foundation that future generations can emulate and expand upon, empowering them to carry the torch of purpose forward.

I have always told my children that I would rather they have well-lived lives rather than a life in pursuit of happiness. Happiness is a temporary state that ebbs and flows with the ups and downs of life. Abraham Lincoln said, "[Most people are] about as happy as [they] make up their mind to be." A life well-lived includes finding and fulfilling your purpose and, in the process, having a positive impact on others and finding true JOY, a lifelong mindset that is found in a personal relationship with your Creator.

MAKING A MARK

Mark Anderson, my neighbor across the street, was one of the finest people I have ever known. He was always willing to help, share, and provide legal input on any issue that came up. He was a trial attorney, and he drafted a new will for Tamela and me.

He was also a skilled craftsman and was constantly working on projects in his garage directly across the street from my office window. I knew it was a Saturday morning when I heard his trusty table saw running on the next DIY project he and his wife had planned. They were never-ending, and every now and then, he'd give us a tour of the house to show us what they'd done. We were amazed at the changes—they had replaced all their stairs with wood, shiplapped the upstairs living room, completely finished the basement with a bar, game room, full bathroom, and movie theater, and added a door that led to the backyard from a look-out basement.

They had an inground swimming pool installed, literally turning their whole backyard into an oasis, complete with a tiki bar and sound system. It wasn't uncommon for Mark to drop by and invite everyone over for an impromptu neighborhood bash.

There was a day I decided to apply a chemical wipe to my aging shutters that was supposed to make them look like new. The smell was so strong when I opened the package that I almost passed out, and you had to wear special gloves to hold the wipes, so only heaven knows what substance they were soaked in. But they really did work. However, when it was time to work on the second story, I needed to borrow a taller ladder. I walked over to ask to borrow Mark's ladder, not only did he loan it to me, he came along with me and insisted on holding the ladder for me. I insisted that I would be fine, but he was adamant. This is the type of guy he was—even though he was busy with his latest project when I walked over, he dropped everything to spend a good hour or more helping me with mine, totally unsolicited.

We also had an annual bet. Whichever of our football teams won (Packers for me, Vikings for him), we had to blow out and shovel the other person's driveway. I'm happy to report that more often than not, he was the one clearing out my driveway. But he didn't need a bet to do a good deed; on many occasions, he blew out our driveway and a few others just because he was up earlier than the rest of us. He also blew out the sidewalk all the way down to the corner and back, city property not his own, just so the kids didn't have to trudge through the snow to get on the bus. He was always willing to go the extra mile for anyone and never had to be asked to do it.

Over the years, I learned he was from South Dakota, grew up in agriculture, and realized that wasn't what he wanted to do. He had a wide-ranging resume, including running the finance department for a large Minnesota car dealer, but ultimately decided he wanted to go to law school. He got his start a little later than most but completed all his studies, passed the bar, and opened his own firm. He dealt with a wide variety of clients and had a very solid, successful practice.

Unfortunately, we lost Mark at only fifty-seven years of age. To this day, he is still missed by everyone— his family and the neighborhood alike. The greatest tribute to the difference he made was the sheer number of people who attended his celebration of life service. His wife, Gerri, shared with me that neither she nor the children had ever met a number of the people who came through the receiving line. Yet, each person shared stories of how Mark had done something for them they never forgot, considered him a friend, and felt compelled to come and share those stories with the family.

Mark's life was a shining example of someone who lived life as a servant leader and discovered his true purpose later in life. While he had always loved helping others, practicing law became the ultimate expression of his calling. Well done, Mark Anderson!

FROM GANGS TO GLORY

Early on in our direct-selling business venture, we met Derrick Agate. Originally from Jamaica, he grew up on the eastern seaboard, where his mom worked hard to give her children a better life in America. Unfortunately, he found himself with the wrong crowd (i.e., gangs). As "D" says, they almost got him—and would have if it hadn't been for "coach."

Derrick is a gentle giant and was quickly identified as a potentially great wrestler. Coach recruited him onto his team in middle school, and when he learned of Derrick's home life difficulties and the constant pull toward the gangs, he offered Derrick to move in with him. That move completely changed the direction of Derrick's life and also led him to a relationship with Jesus.

Derrick invited Tamela and me to come to his church in Eden Prairie, and as I got to know him, I learned that he and his wife Kim were doing the same thing his coach had done for him: inviting young men to live with their growing family and getting them involved in wrestling and church, living the phrase "paying it forward!"

He's also very entrepreneurial and, in addition to selling school buses in retirement, he has successfully developed, produced, and promoted his own brand of barbeque sauce called Jamaican Jerk that you can now find on the shelves of many of the area's Twin Cities Hy-Vee stores. In the summer months, he and his family team can be found at a variety of events promoting Jamaican Jerk. Derrick is truly living his life on purpose.

BEYOND THE COURT

Another example of a person whose life was well-lived is Wayman Tisdale. Son of an Oklahoma pastor, Tisdale grew up in a churchgoing, athletic, and musical family. He called music his first love, playing the bass at his father's church, and was able to dunk a basketball in the eighth grade.

Over a twelve-year period, he played professional ball for the Indiana Pacers, Sacramento Kings, and Phoenix Suns. He won a gold medal as a part of the 1984 Men's Olympic Games under head coach Bobby Knight, the first gold medal-winning American basketball team with amateur players.

Tisdale recalled, "I had some coaches that literally didn't want me to make it, and one in particular was Bobby Knight. At the time I frowned on that … I look at it today that had I not persevered through a lot of the stuff he put me through, I probably wouldn't be here today. I thank God for that dude because he pushed me."

He retired in 1997 to focus on his music career. There were two things that made Tisdale's music so unique. First, he chose smooth jazz as his genre instead of rap, which was the common choice of so many other professional athletes. Second, he brought to mainstream music the style/sound of bass guitar as the lead instrument, like the electric lead guitar that carries the melody line in the song—a style that is now very popular in today's smooth jazz world. Tisdale released his first album, Power Forward, in 1995 as a nod to his position as a ball player, and he recorded seven more albums before his untimely death from bone cancer in 2009 at age forty-four.

According to a note in the album sleeve, the song "Bright" by guitarist Peter White (Good Day, 2009) was dedicated "to the memory of Wayman Tisdale, whose spirit never failed to brighten our lives." White said, "The guy was always so happy, so positive, always had a smile, always made you feel great. Even before his death, I'd always called this song 'Bright,' because it sounded uplifting and happy and funny. Then I realized that it would be the perfect song to dedicate to Wayman because that was the way he came across to the world." Here's to a life filled with purpose and clearly well-lived, Wayman Tisdale!

UNSHAKABLE RESILIENCE

Another hometown hero in Tamela's and my life is Condello (it's a Greek name and she goes by Dello) Hostetler, who we met through involvement in our direct-selling business. She has become a dear family friend, but just as important, a person of great resilience.

Over the time we have known Dello, she and her husband Mike have dealt with very tough financial times. Mike developed Parkinson's disease and passed away about five years ago. We'd run into her while they were going through all of this, but you'd never know it. She always had a smile, would ask questions about you and your family and remained very focused on others.

In addition to that, she has maintained a very successful direct-selling business, helped her son launch several successful businesses, never misses any of her many grandchildren's games and activities, supports and stays in touch with her many friends and keeps a youthful spirit and can-do approach to all she does. When you ask Dello how she does it all, she simply smiles and replies, "I know I'm in the exact right place, doing exactly what I am supposed to be doing with my life." I submit that is a textbook definition of living a life on purpose!

—

As we come to the close of this journey through the power of purpose, I want to leave you with one final thought: Purpose is not a destination but a way of life. It is not a single moment of clarity that defines us but a collection of actions, decisions, and reflections that shape who we are and who we become. Whether it's the legacy we create for our families, the service we give to others, or the quiet ways we contribute to the world, living with purpose provides meaning, direction, and a sense of fulfillment that transcends the fleeting nature of happiness.

Like the stories of Mark, Derrick, Wayman, Dello, and the others who have been featured in these pages, we are all called to make an impact—not through grand gestures or fame but through our daily choices, relationships, and acts of service. Purpose is found in the small moments and in the big ones. It is about living authentically, without apology, and with the confidence that the path we are walking is the one we were meant to travel.

What I am hoping we have accomplished together is a really solid start in helping you figure out your true purpose in life so you can move forward living your best life. Ask yourself: What legacy do I want to leave? How will my actions today impact the world and the people around me? And, most importantly, are you living a life that truly aligns with who you are, who you were created to be, and the good you can bring into the world?

I don't have all the answers, but I do know that a life well-lived is a life of purpose, and that is something we can all strive for. The choice is yours: to live with intention, to make a difference, and to create a legacy that lasts. Let that be your guiding light as you continue your own journey, and may your purpose shine brightly for generations to come.

NOTES

_____

_____

_____

_____

_____

_____

_____

_____

_____

RECOMMENDED READING LIST

There have been so many books that have helped me discover and develop my purpose. Whether I have been working toward identifying my core values, examining my habits, learning from the successes of others, or strengthening my mindset, the below books have helped me evolve and have fueled my growth mindset. Take a look and try a few!

1. *How to Win Friends and Influence People* by Dale Carnegie
2. *Atomic Habits* by James Clear
3. *The Magic of Thinking Big* by David J. Schwartz
4. *How to Stop Worrying and Start Living* by Dale Carnegie
5. *Who Moved My Cheese?* by Spencer Johnson
6. *The 360 Degree Leader* by John C. Maxwell
7. *The Power of Positive Thinking* by Norman Vincent Peale

8. *Rich Dad Poor Dad* by Robert T. Kiyosaki

9. *Attitude 101* by John C. Maxwell

10. *The Purpose Driven Life* by Rick Warren

11. *Getting Things Done* by David Allen

12. *The Five Love Languages* by Gary Chapman

13. *The 7 Habits of Highly Effective People* by Stephen R. Covey

14. *Daring Greatly* by Brené Brown

15. *Failing Forward* by John C. Maxwell

16. *23 Minutes in Hell* by Bill Wiese

17. *The Case for Christ* by Lee Strobel

18. *I Don't Have Enough Faith to be an Atheist* by Norman L. Geisler

19. *The Precious Present* by Spencer Johnson

20. *Thinking for a Change* by John C. Maxwell

This list is just a place to start. Remember, leaders are readers!

NOTES

_____

_____

_____

_____

_____

AN INVITATION

I am a sinner saved by grace. I have put my faith and trust in my living Savior, Jesus Christ. He took my place on the cross so that I could spend eternity–a really long time–in Heaven with God.

If you've never accepted an invitation to invite Christ into your life, it's very simple. Just pray this prayer:

"LORD JESUS, FORGIVE ME OF MY SINS AND COME
INTO MY HEART. I MAKE YOU MY LORD AND SAVIOR.
AMEN."

If you prayed that prayer with a sincere heart, you are saved.

Why should you do this? First, do you know where you will go after you die? If you don't have the same assurance I do—that when my heart beats its last, I will be in the eternal presence of God and His Son, Jesus—please read on and consider accepting this invitation.

Second, in the world we live in today, evil has deliberately worked to remove God from our national consciousness, promoting a culture of lies and half-truths. Why? Because evil is after your soul. Without Jesus as your Savior, you are destined for hell. Maybe you don't believe in hell—but that doesn't change its existence. And by the time you realize the truth, it will be too late to do anything about it.

Think of it this way: You can claim you don't believe in gravity and step off a tall building. But I guarantee, you'll become a believer on the way down.

One of the greatest tactics of evil is to distract your mind with everything that has no eternal significance—things like self, money, possessions, "my truth," sex, instant gratification, entitlement, race, gender, religion, and ignorance, just to name a few. But the Bible clearly states: "No one comes to the Father except through the Son." (John 14:6). You see, it's not about religion—it's about a relationship with our Lord and Savior, Jesus Christ.

Christian author and speaker Bill Wiese offers a powerful analogy to explain this:

> *Imagine you and I drive to the nicest neighborhood in town. We walk up to the most beautiful house, knock on the door, and say, "Hi, I'm Bill, and this is Mitch. We'd like to live here!" Before, during, or after calling the police, the homeowner would say, "I'm sorry, but I don't know you."*

Without a personal relationship with Jesus Christ, God will one day say the same thing: "I don't know you." (Matthew 7:23).

Third, I believe—and have personally experienced—that everyone is walking around with a God-sized hole in their heart, a void that only a relationship with

Him, made possible through His Son, Jesus Christ, can fill. If you feel like something is missing in your life, that no amount of success, money, love, sex, power, or possessions can satisfy, that's the Holy Spirit calling you into a relationship with God through Jesus.

Since Adam and Eve sinned, sin has been passed down through every generation, and its exponential growth is why the world is in such a mess. It's also the reason Jesus had to be born of a virgin—incarnate by the Holy Spirit—so that the seed of sin was not in Him. God, being perfect and just, will not allow sin into Heaven. That's why Satan and his followers were cast out.

Because sin separates us from God, we cannot enter Heaven on our own. You might say, *"Well, I'm a good person, and I do good things!"* That may be true, but are you perfect? *"What? Of course not!"* Exactly. None of us are. We are all on the same playing field because no one is perfect—but perfection is God's standard.

So how do we measure up? The truth is, we can't. And God, in His infinite wisdom, knew this.

What was God's solution? He sent Himself to do the job for us and offered His salvation as a free gift! How? By sending His only Son. Jesus Christ, fully human yet fully God, is the author and finisher of our faith. His death on the cross, His descent into hell to claim victory over death, and His resurrection serve as the perfect atonement for the sins of the world. When you accept Jesus as your personal Savior, His atonement makes you perfect in God's eyes. He fully paid the price for our sins because we could never do it on our own. That is love beyond our ability to comprehend.

What is the single best piece of evidence we have to examine and investigate all of this? The Bible. It consists of sixty-six books written by more than forty different authors, each inspired by the Holy Spirit. These authors came from all walks of life—shepherds, farmers, tentmakers, physicians, fishermen, philosophers, and kings—spanning a period of 1,500 years, from around 1450 BC (the time of Moses) to about AD 100 (following the death and resurrection of Jesus Christ).

Additionally, the Bible has been canonized, meaning it has been measured against the highest standard of divine inspiration and historical accuracy. For centuries, archaeologists have relied on the Bible as a guide to uncover buildings, people, places, and civilizations, repeatedly confirming its historical reliability.

The Bible is also filled with over 300 prophecies specifically about one person—Jesus. He not only appeared but fulfilled every single one of them! Statistically, the probability of one person fulfilling just eight of these prophecies is like covering the entire state of Texas with silver dollars, two feet deep, marking one with a red dot, and picking that exact coin on the first try. Now imagine fulfilling all 300! It would be impossible—unless He is God.

Perhaps the most compelling evidence comes from His apostles. Every one of them, except John, died a martyr's death. These were the same men who, after Jesus' crucifixion, ran and hid in fear for their lives. What changed? They encountered the risen Jesus. Would you willingly die for a lie? Would they? Of course not. Their unwavering faith, even unto death, speaks volumes.

It's not my job to convince you; that's the Holy Spirit's role. My job is simply to encourage you to investigate this truth for yourself. There is no greater gift I could offer than this message. Your life—both now and for eternity—is in your hands. The choice is yours.

ABOUT THE AUTHOR

MITCH LARSON is a Wisconsin native who grew up primarily in Eau Claire, experiencing all the Midwestern charm the area has to offer. His career path took him to Northern Minnesota and the Minneapolis/St. Paul area, where he has spent most of his adult working life. His personal and professional experiences have led him to recognize the importance of purpose in everyone's life, which inspired him to write this book.

As an avid reader of self-development literature, Mitch aimed to create a book that equips readers with the essential tools to develop and live your life on purpose. In this book, you will not only learn valuable life lessons from his experiences and reflections, but you will also be encouraged to examine your own life, reflect on your experiences, and ultimately discover and cultivate your true purpose.

www.ingramcontent.com/pod-product-compliance
Lightning Source LLC
Chambersburg PA
CBHW041142120626
46547CB00020B/3077